A PRIMER ON CHIEFS AND CHIEFDOMS

PRINCIPLES OF ARCHAEOLOGY

A PRIMER ON CHIEFS AND CHIEFDOMS

TIMOTHY EARLE
Northwestern University
Evanston, Illinois

ELIOT WERNER PUBLICATIONS, INC.
CLINTON CORNERS, NEW YORK

Library of Congress Cataloging-in-Publication Data

Names: Earle, Timothy K., author.
Title: A primer on chiefs and chiefdoms / Timothy Earle, Northwestern
  University, Evanston Illinois.
Description: Clinton Corners, New York : Eliot Werner Publications, Inc.,
  [2021] | Series: Principles of archaeology | Includes bibliographical
  references.
Identifiers: LCCN 2020049922| ISBN 9781734281835 (paperback) | ISBN
  9781734281842 (epub) | ISBN 9781734281859 (pdf)
Subjects: LCSH: Chiefdoms--History. | Human evolution. | Economics—
  Political aspects.
Classification: LCC GN492.55 .E27 2021 | DDC 306.2--dc23
LC record available at https://lccn.loc.gov/2020049922

ISBN-10: 1-7342818-3-9
ISBN-13: 978-1-7342818-3-5

Printed in the United States of America

To Andres Moya Castro of Ataura in the Mantaro Valley—
UMARP team member, local authority, solver of all
problems, and dear friend

PROLOGUE

Historical science of politics is the one science that is deposited by the
streams of history, like the grains of gold in the sand of a river; and the
knowledge of the past, the record of truths revealed . . . is eminently
practical, as an instrument of action and a power that goes to making
the future.
(Dalberg-Acton 1895, p. 3)

What is it about chiefdoms? They are traditional societies and many might
inquire about their relevance for our modern world. In this book I
argue that studying chiefdoms is essential to understand the role of elemental
powers in social evolution. Anthropological archaeology is a social science
able to study comparatively the natural experiments of long-term historical
processes. To illustrate this point, I look at chiefs and their power strategies
in historically independent prehistoric and traditional societies and discuss
how they continue to exist as powerful actors within states.

Who are chiefs? They are political operatives holding titles of leadership
over groups larger than intimate kin-based communities. They rule with some
consent of their group, but they are all about building personal power and respect. They are inherently highly variable. Sometimes I refer to chiefs as chieftains. Although these terms are largely interchangeable, I use the terms
somewhat differently to designate relative variations in institutional versus
personal power. Chieftains are more self-made leaders and chiefs are more institutional leaders, but all chief-like leaders come to power and perpetuate
power as conjoined political processes.

My engagement with chiefdoms has been long. I went to college in the
mid-1960s when student activism was on the rise. It was time for revolution,
we thought. We anticipated major progress for racial integration, world peace,
ending social injustice, and erasing income inequality. As did many of the six-
ties generation, I was easily radicalized and questioned authority. My determination to understand our political system encouraged me to become an
anthropologist and raise the question of why people would follow leaders,
often against their own interests.

Power corrupts and progressive movements depend on ways to tame
chiefs. We can build on humanity's better instincts to fashion order that balances human needs and interests. But how is this possible? Comparative stud-

ies of human societies propose alternative institutional formations and their implications for human justice and sustainability. Throughout my academic career, my optimism has been rooted in archaeology and its perspective on deep history. Here the quotation by Lord Acton is relevant: history (archaeology) offers a social science of political institutions, which includes the lessons that chiefdoms tell.

CHIEFDOMS

Chiefdoms are the first societies with institutional leaders. Many scholars have viewed chiefs as problem solvers—defending groups against aggressors, resolving disputes, providing support under hardship, organizing labor for community projects, and redistributing goods among those in need. Chiefs do these things, but much of what chiefs do is to accumulate benefits for themselves, staying in power and legitimizing control. Chiefly supporters pledge undying support in return for guarantees of payoffs.

Perhaps this sounds familiar. With the evolution of state societies, chiefs have become partly domesticated by the rule of law, but their presence is still visible everywhere—from business entrepreneurs to urban drug lords to local politicians. The challenge of modern societies is to domesticate the entrepreneurial spirit of chiefs to the rule of law that channels their efforts for the broader good. Is this feasible? Based on lessons from the past, I think it is.

THERE IS NO END TO HISTORY

Although present conditions (whether poverty, power, or environmental warming) may appear inevitable, societies continually change—often for the better but too frequently for the worst. There is no end to history and archaeology offers key insights. Human societies have been incredibly variable and creative; social and economic conditions are never predetermined. We can understand what is possible and the outcomes of one political system compared with others as recorded in prehistory.

Archaeology documents long-term processes with opportunities to understand and create alternative pathways for change. Over the last twenty thousand years, human have built vastly larger and more diverse societies and centralized political power has strengthened, but has also relaxed. During the twentieth century, for example, the apparent imperial destiny of world powers (Britain, France, Germany, Japan, and the Soviet Union) expanded only to collapse. States now stand under the full gaze of world criticism. We are learning better how humans organize at different scales.

These social scales have distinct and often competing interests and capabilities. History shows how balance is possible with powers shifting back and forth. Prehistoric societies offer opportunities to study the implications of a wide range of human organizations. Finding the correct balance between scale and organization (family, community, region, and state) is an empirical question for which history provides alternative resolutions.

ARCHAEOLOGY IS A SOCIAL SCIENCE

Archaeology is a social science able to discover long-term principles and consequences of human actions. With a sweeping increase in archaeology's capabilities to describe social systems in action, we are able to use large data sets to uncover alternative pathways by which humans have organized themselves and the outcomes of those natural experiments.

No longer is archaeology simply the recovery of the oldest this or the origin of that. It has the potential for systematic scientific understanding of human societies as a means to help fashion future policy directions. To match our increasing methodological capability, we need sophisticated theory to guide our research. Linking theoretically to political economy, recent archaeological work considers political ecology, meaning simply the ways in which human societies create anthropogenic environments—some destined for degradation and collapse while others are sustainable over the long haul.

To enable an archaeology relevant to modern problems of change and stability, we should continue the work archaeologists have always done—finding, excavating, and analyzing material evidence and its changing patterning in the past. We must take the past as fundamentally knowable, developing new ways of recovery and conceptualization of historical conditions. Have leaders helped solve human challenges or have they been an emerging problem channeling resources to their personal benefits? These are fundamental questions that archaeology is well equipped to investigate with the study of chiefdoms and their leadership institutions.

ACKNOWLEDGMENTS

To understand chiefdoms a lifetime of collaborations, discussions, and reading with many anthropologists, historical sociologists, and political scientists have guided my career. I look to my intellectual "ancestors" including Robert Carneiro, Colin Renfrew, Marshall Sahlins, Roy Rappaport, and Eric Wolf. These professors and friends formed my approach to social evolution and the emergence of strong leaders.

I did graduate work at the University of Michigan, where my fellow graduate students and I created a cohort with common theoretical interests that pioneered new approaches to archaeological research. These included especially Elizabeth Brumfiel, Gary Feinman, Antonio Gilman, Allen Johnson,

Patrick Kirch, and Kristian Kristiansen. My own graduate students at UCLA and Northwestern have provided daily interactions in seminars, discussions, and fieldwork that have always been central to my career. I think especially of Luis Jaime Castillo, Terence D'Altroy, Elizabeth DeMarrais, Christine Hastorf, and John Steinberg. They always knew how to speak to authority, keeping me honest and current with new ideas and approaches.

The evidence that supports the argument of this primer comes from many sources, including anthropology's rich ethnographic record and the mounting archaeological record of chiefdoms. I do not cite individual sources in the text, but they are credited in each chapter in the Additional Readings section; each source has a detailed bibliography.

I draw heavily on my personal field projects in the Pacific (Hawaiian Islands), the Andes (Peru and Argentina), and Europe (Denmark and Hungary). Full summer field seasons in these countries have offered excitement and reward from different cultures, peoples, and landscapes. In each field project, I have been embedded within large teams of scholars, students, and workers laboring together. I hold particular affection for the skilled non-academics upon whom I depended for their labor, personal skills, local knowledge, and insights. The community members in the Mantaro, Thy, and the Benta made my work possible.

From 1967 to 2008, the National Science Foundation funded my research—first as an undergraduate participant and then as a graduate student and senior scholar across five major archaeological projects. I am deeply grateful for this support; the many reviewers who sharpened my research; and John Yellen, the longtime director of NSF's Archaeology Program who nurtured my science-based approach bringing together a strong theoretical perspective with carefully designed, data-driven research. I have learned that my ideas can be usefully wrong, as field results correct my theories and point me in new directions of thinking and practicing. Details of the extensive financial support of my field projects are found in my publications.

This primer stands as something of an intellectual biography, for which the support and understanding of my family is central. In 1967 I met my wife Eliza as an undergraduate on an archaeological project in Arizona, and after marrying in 1969 she accompanied me on many of my field excavations—endlessly discussing my ideas and providing basic support mapping, preparing illustrations, digging, and washing sherds, My daughters learned to think like archaeologists, working with me in Argentina and Denmark and always ready with pointed advice. Perhaps most importantly my family listened with excitement to my rambling ideas and commented thoughtfully on my writings. Why should I be so lucky?

Eliot Werner invited me to write about the study of chiefdoms and as his reward has had to work tirelessly to realize the book. I am particular grateful for his help and also to Gary Feinman, whose insightful and timely guidance helped me see what was needed.

CONTENTS

A PRIMER ON CHIEFS AND CHIEFDOMS

CHAPTER 1

CHIEFDOM ETHNOGRAPHIES OF POWER AND AUTHORITY

To begin our study of chiefdoms, we discuss some definitions related to intermediate-level societies; each concept has a history of different usages and meaning but still captures fundamental characteristics of regional polities. I want to emphasize that chiefs and their chiefdoms are highly variable—reflecting specifics of histories, environments, subsistence practices and technologies, interregional relations, and sources of power.

Having said this, the processes involved in the formation of chiefdoms across many cases show common patterns based on their political economies. To understand these political processes, I adopt broad categories of chiefs and chiefdoms that share elements of social stratification and power differentials.

CHIEFDOMS AS POLITICAL SOCIETIES

Chiefdoms were political societies, meaning that they had leaders able to coordinate political action with thousands or even tens of thousands of people. Typically, chiefdoms regionally organized multiple village-sized communities, although single communities with large populations could also be so structured. To integrate regional-scale polities required social, economic, religious, and especially political institutions. Chiefdoms were (and still are) about power, the ability to influence and coerce groups with divergent interests and identities. Chiefdoms represented a spectrum of political formations.

Power is fundamentally distributive—all humans have power to act independently, if only not to act when ordered. This is what allows both families and communities to operate quite autonomously of their chiefs for much of everyday life. As parents quickly learn, even within families and despite authority hierarchies based on age, physical size, and nominal control, much of the time children do exactly what they want despite parental orders. A strong human principle is anarchy: individuals, families, and communities follow their own inclinations. Everyone can claim powers and the

1

easiest way to direct others is to provide them with things they desire. Political relationships are always a balance between individuals and their perceptions of advantages, if only to escape punishment.

Power can manifests itself in potential mastery over others, asking for sacrifice for the broader good. Power is thus not a resource but rather an unequal relationship; power implies threats, unequal rewards, and certainly resistance. Unequal relations are formed out of various media that include knowledge, social structure, warrior might, economy, and ritual ideology. Power relationships are always present but inherently problematic. How chiefs come to power in some situations and not in others is an enduring question of anthropology and one that archaeologists are well suited to answer.

CHIEFS

Chiefs are political operatives acting to further group interests but always with their own interests at heart. They design power strategies to amass and extend control over populations larger than intimate, village-scale communities. By providing goods and services for their subjects, chiefs bind people to their group. Chiefs resolve internal disputes, host ceremonial feasts, organize defense, and build ceremonial places, agricultural systems, and defensive works. Coercively, chiefs can punish individuals and communities that resist their authority.

Marshall Sahlins defined differences between the "Big Man" of Melanesia and the Polynesian chief according to the scale, stability, and institutionalization of political leadership. A Big Man is a political entrepreneur who personally builds power by amassing prestige; by contrast, a chief comes to a leadership position within an established political structure. These processes are additive in the sense that the chief does the same thing that a Big Man must do to build his power, but he works within an institutional order that legitimizes the chief's role.

Chiefs seek to differentiate themselves from the rest of society in terms of rank, authority, power, and the gleam of leadership. Sahlins's binary division actually represented a continuum of leadership forms signifying dialectical tensions between groups and their leaders. Within the inherently competitive world of chiefdoms, chiefs create and extend their support base through a highly personalized network—not unlike a Big Man. Big Men grade into chiefs, who grade into state actors (sultans, kings, and emperors) to the extent that they are able to expand scales of control over the political economy and stabilize sovereignty through institutions of governance.

Chiefs develop power strategies that bring together pragmatic mixtures of economic, warrior, and religious means to build and maintain followers. Sometimes chiefs attract followers through economic services or religious ritual; in other cases they coerce followers by threats and punishment. The particular mix in a power strategy changes over time and often fails as chiefs lose the power they have sought to monopolize. As I seek to show, chiefdoms are not a societal type but a political process seeking some measure of control.

CHIEFTAINCIES

Chieftaincies are political institutions with highly personalized networks of specialized agents supporting some semblance of centralized rule; they are political machines designed to create, legitimize, and hold sovereignty. Chieftaincies include chiefly power specialists consisting of warriors, priests, managers, and others involved in the collection and defense of revenues that support the chief's power strategies. Their personal loyalty to the chief is critical. This loyalty is reinforced by expectations of personal gain.

Chiefs operate like modern oligarchs who surround themselves with loyal retinues of lawyers, facilitators, accountants, and personal security to defend their patron's wealth and well-being. Although frequently based on principles of kinship and rank, chieftaincies are better understood as personalized relationships of fealty (see, for example, descriptions of European feudalism). Chieftaincies have variable institutional structures with more or less established social hierarchies, corporate ownership of resources, organized warfare, and rituals. Chieftaincies are built, maintained, and materialized by gift exchanges. By controlling the distribution of land and wealth, chiefs provide incentives to stay loyal. With competitive warfare between chiefs, members of a losing chieftaincy lose everything—often including their lives.

CHIEFDOMS

Chiefdoms organize regional societies with political, economic, and ritual institutions. They vary in size from simple chiefdoms of a few thousand to institutionally more complex systems with tens of thousands of subjects. Chiefdoms have little coherence as a type, except for their flexible power strategies to mobilize revenues from their communities and abroad, and inherently can fracture into smaller units (as described ethnographically for segmentary societies).

Chiefdoms are essentially tribal; typically, they are ethnically homogeneous but with a measure of social hierarchy and political centrality. The political and social hierarchy is routinely grounded in patterns of resource ownership for which chiefs claim rights to surpluses of goods and labor from constituencies. Multiple hierarchies can exist simultaneously at different scales and different spheres of action (social relations, political networks, warriors, and religion). Chiefdoms usually involve warfare for defending productive land and other resources—conquering land often with capital facilities and farmers and raiding for wealth and slaves.

Chiefdoms are multiscalar organizations. They are organizations of families embedded in local communities, which are in turn part of regional polities (political institutions). At each level individuals operate to further their own perceived interests. In many ways everyday lives of families and communities within chiefdoms continue unchanged from more egalitarian and decentralized societies. Chiefs concern themselves largely with chiefly things that supplement existing organizations, and constituent groups run their lives autonomously—except in situations where chiefs require labor or services from their followers or followers receive specific services.

CHIEFLY CONFEDERACIES

Chiefly confederacies are alliances of chieftaincies. They are pragmatic and ever-changing associations typically involving transient coalitions, intermarriages, and mobility among specialists (warriors, priests, architects, and the like). Chiefly confederacies are an additional scalar organizational layer. They are inherently contingent and based on common interests between chiefs, which shift quickly. They are thus unstable, forming and dissolving opportunistically according to changing strategic openings and interests in the political arena. Confederacies have no permanent institutional form but they can create broad political relationships (typically reliant on warfare) that can appear almost empire-like, in which multiple chiefs and their chieftaincy pledge support—for as long as it lasts—to a paramount leader.

THE USE OF ETHNOGRAPHIES

To understand chiefdoms I start by looking at societies described ethnographically by anthropologists. This approach assumes that archaeology documents human organizational forms that were likely represented by societies existing into the modern era. To comprehend how prehistoric societies operated, archaeologists need to be conversant with world ethnographies of traditional societies studied by nineteenth and twentieth century sociocultural anthropologists. The ethnographic record is anthropology's great legacy to understand and appreciate the extraordinary diversity in human societies.

To grasp the feel of chiefdoms, I summarize some classic ethnographies and cover cases at different political scales from Polynesia, Africa, Southeast Asia, and the Caribbean (Figure 1.1). Chiefdoms on different continents around the world were historically separated from each other until after European colonial

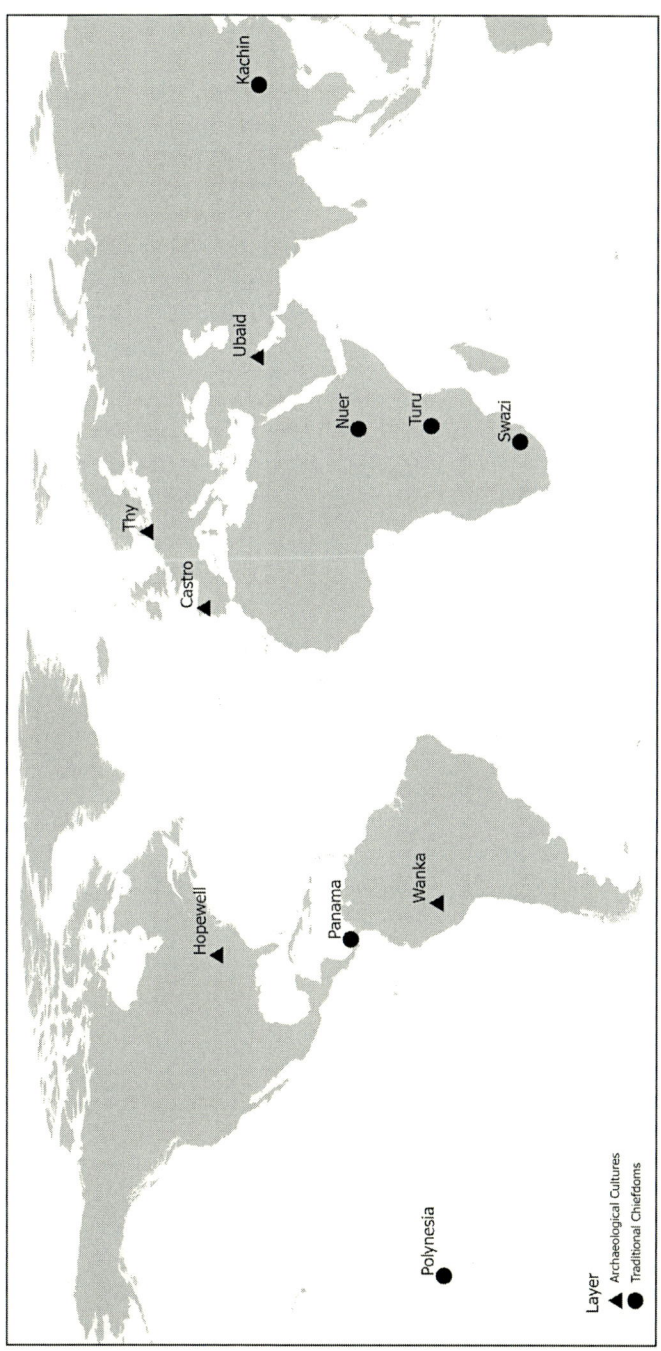

Figure 1.1. World map showing locations of the chiefdoms (circles = ethnographic cases; triangles = archaeological cases) considered in this book. Illustration prepared by Mark Hauser.

expansion. This section illustrates the diversity of intermediate-scale societies for which we have good historical descriptions by anthropologists, and I hope future students of archaeology will enjoy reading ethnographies to understand human societies in the past and present.

PACIFIC ISLAND CHIEFDOMS

Polynesian societies offer exceptional examples of chiefdoms that survived into the ethnographic present—the time when anthropologists first described them. Starting several thousand years ago, Polynesians created a distinctive canoe technology with a sail design that allowed them to voyage deep into the Pacific. In one of the remarkable examples of human maritime colonization, these skilled mariners explored the isolated Pacific islands that previously had no human occupation. They colonized all inhabitable lands in the Polynesian triangle, from Tikopia to Easter Island and from the Hawaiian Islands on the north to the temperate islands of New Zealand on the south (Figure 1.2).

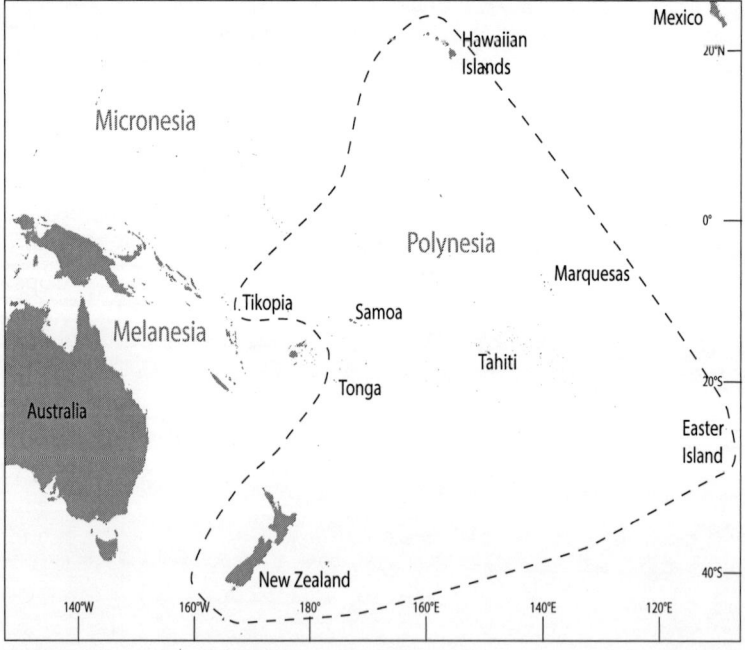

Figure 1.2. The Polynesian triangle of island archipelagoes in the deep Pacific, east of Australia and west of the Americas. The islands were settled from Melanesia and occupied historically by Polynesian chiefdoms. Illustration prepared by Mark Hauser.

Historically, Polynesians are a single people with closely related languages and cultures. The islands that they colonized ranged from tiny coral atolls to large high volcanic islands, from isolated islands to large archipelagos, and from the tropics to subtropical and temperate zones. They shared common technologies including irrigated and dryland tuber agriculture; domesticated pigs, chicken, and dogs; fishing technologies of nets and hooks; a mixture of weapons and working tools; and simple grass-frame housing. They also shared common principles of kinship and social hierarchy. All Polynesians had chiefs but their power was highly variable.

Because of the spatial separation of Oceania's archipelagoes, each island group developed largely in isolation. Polynesia can thus be seen as a laboratory for the study of cultural adaptation. Its history and prehistory document adaptive radiation of a single cultural form to diverse economic and political opportunities. When originally finding a new island, the colonizing group formed a fairly open, small-scale society that evolved through various political outcomes—from essentially egalitarian Tikopia to the more typical Marquesan societies. These independent histories were separate adaptations, which were guided by prospects of each island group for surplus production and the ability to control mobilization to support chiefly polities. The full potential represented by Polynesia is illustrated by the Hawaiian Island chiefdoms, which developed state-like characteristics based on engineered landscapes and conquest warfare (see Chapter 6).

With population growth, groups became heavily dependent on tuber and tree agriculture, animal husbandry (especially pigs), and fishing. Agricultural facilities differed especially according to environmental conditions. These improvements have been called landesque capital, meaning simply that individual families and communities invested their labor to intensify fields for sustainable, long-term yields. Farming exemplifies simple landesque capital, whereby individual families worked to enrich soils and plant tree crops. This labor investment included soil augmentations such as mulching, extensive agricultural terracing, and highly productive irrigation systems. Such capital improvements increased productivity since it bound people to their farm plots. Irrigated taro and other forms of agricultural intensification were common throughout Polynesia.

Variation also existed in the extent and nature of trade and warfare. Where island groups were much isolated from each other, trade was of little importance. Thus trade between islands was minimal for the Hawaiian Islands but more important for other groups with closely clustered islands, such as Tonga and Samoa.

Warfare to defend local communities and their built landscapes was common across Polynesia. Although settlement patterns were occasionally focused on fortified villages (for instance, in New Zealand), households were often scattered along the beaches and among the fields. The development of regional chiefdoms appears to have resulted from conquest warfare, organized by chiefs to extend power over multiple communities and guarantee peace among the constituent communities.

Structurally, the basic social and economic unit was patrilineal-ranked lineage that formed a local community owning land corporately. With a substrate of ranking, local communities had hereditary chiefs from senior lineages and these chiefs were always important ritually and often functioned in other spheres. The Polynesian principle of ranking created a measured distance in status and prerogative from senior lines. Historically specific to this culture area, such ranking created structural conditions for the formation of social hierarchies.

The rich ethnographic and ethnohistorical studies of Polynesia provided what became archetypical examples of chiefdoms. Polynesian chiefdoms, however, were highly variable, adjusting to local conditions and histories. Furthermore, the extreme isolation of Pacific island archipelagoes actually generated quite atypical historical conditions for social evolution—namely, extreme social circumscription making control rather easy, little trade, and no markets. Polynesian chiefdoms were thus quite unusual and should not be considered typical of how chiefdoms developed and operated.

Tikopia

Tikopia is one end of a spectrum of Polynesian political complexity. It is a small outlier island west of the Polynesian triangle and just north of the Melanesian islands of Vanuatu. British ethnographer Raymond Firth described its society and economy in the late 1920s. Tikopia is an eroded volcanic cone of about five square kilometers standing isolated in the sea. When studied by Firth, the population was less than 1,300, dispersed in twenty or so scattered but named permanent settlements with associated land.

Subsistence was based on dryland farming (especially of taro) with fields on slopes, tree crops (breadfruit and coconuts) on flats, and fishing (net and line, often using canoes). Because no streams existed, irrigation was very small scale and depended on a few springs. The island's high population density required intensive farming with short fallow and mulching. Because Tikopia was so isolated, its products were little desired and long-distance canoes were lacking. Trade was minimal and Tikopia was mainly self-sufficient.

Tikopia was a typical Polynesian society with ranked lineages that were residential in a particular location. Lineages (called "houses" in Firth's original account) owned land, orchards, and canoes. Warfare traditionally existed between segments that divided the northern and southern areas. Canoes were small and constructed of poor local wood. They could be manufactured and used for fishing by commoners and chiefs alike. Ritual canoes, however, were somewhat special; according to Firth, "They are built by the commoners' own resources and at their initiative; and they themselves used then. The function of the chief is to act as titular owner and perform the principal ritual for them" (1936, p. 218).

A few lineages were senior chiefly lines and their leaders maintained some prerogatives. Chiefly lines owned springs and more orchards than commoners, but agricultural practices created few opportunities for control that could generate surplus to support social stratification. The primary role of the chief was ritual, involved in providing touches to ceremonies—like the ritual drink *kava*—and encouraging surplus agricultural production for feasts. In brief, although some structural elements of hierarchy existed, chiefly power on Tikopia was limited to ritual performance.

The Marquesas

Marquesan chiefdoms are rather typical Polynesian societies. The Marquesas consist of fifteen islands with a total land area of a thousand square kilometers located about 1,400 kilometers northeast of Tahiti. The islands have a romantic image in western art, being the final home of Paul Gauguin—whose paintings captured the mystery and beauty of Polynesia—and the locale for Herman Melville's ethnographic novel *Typee*. The islands are steep volcanic peaks up to 1,200 meters in elevation. They are geologically old and deeply dissected with narrow valleys and limited alluvial soil for farming. The coasts are rugged cliffs with small bays at stream mouths, no fringing flatland, and only small reefs. Habitable zones are limited and isolated.

The islands were first colonized circa 1000 CE and remained isolated from the world economy until they were "discovered" by a Spanish navigator in 1595 and subsequently seized by the French in the nineteenth century. The population has been estimated to have risen to over fifty thousand at contact, a large size for Polynesia but divided into many small groups—often of no more than a thousand people. The primary ethnographic description was by E. S. Craighill Handy, with an excellent study of their elaborate tattooing by his wife W. C. Handy.

The subsistence economy relied heavily on tree crops (breadfruit, coconuts, and bananas) grown along stream bottoms and lower slopes, and on taro grown in small, irrigated terraces along the streams. Pigs, chickens, and dogs were raised in limited numbers. Fishing was primarily offshore using canoes, lines, and nets. Settlements were near the coast and scattered up and down the valley; they formed valley communities but were dispersed and unfortified. Except for some minor trade between valleys and neighboring islands, and externally with distant islands for high-quality adzes, each valley chiefdom was largely economically self-sufficient.

Warfare between valley polities was endemic, with the goal of chiefs to displace local ruling lines and create a regional polity. The beautiful Marquesan war club was a heavy blunt instrument for personal conflict; it was artistically decorated with tattoo-like patterns to create an elaborate prestige object for warriors and chiefs (Figure 1.3). The head of the war club represents a *tiki*, the divine-human figure that symbolized the role of the warrior chief as protector. As shown in the image on the cover, a Marquesan chief held his club to reflect his status—reinforced by his heavy tattooing, which was commonly used throughout Polynesia to exhibit personal power.

The valley polity represented a ranked lineage. Family households were the basic subsistence unit, dependent on their own efforts and technology. Like Tikopia, chiefs were senior lines linked to the gods; commoners were junior lines. Chiefs were recognized as distinctive in prestige but their activities were restricted to ritual, warfare, and some economic matters. They possessed various markers of status—such as elaborate tattooing, war clubs, and serving bowls—fashioned by specialists whom the chiefs sponsored. Chiefly

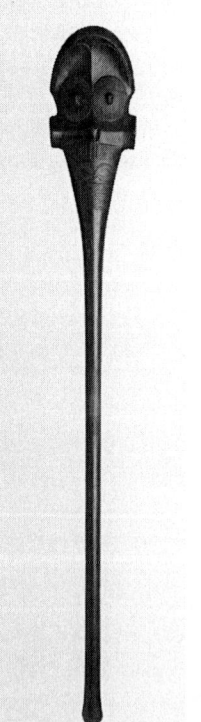

Figure 1.3. A Marquesan war club (*U'u*) with the head representing the *tiki*, a god-human protector. Similar motifs were shown as human tattoos. Gift of the Peabody Academy of Science, 1869. © President and Fellows of Harvard College, Peabody Museum of Archaeology and Ethnology, #PM 69–9–70/1199.

houses were perhaps somewhat larger and better thatched than others but were comparable to commoner houses. Ritual was a chiefly endeavor, involving annual and life crisis ceremonies for chiefly lines. Priests could stand in opposition to chiefs, demanding that chiefs demonstrate legitimacy in warfare.

Warfare was essentially political; chiefs were expected to defend community territory and extend it through conquest. Success demonstrated the gods' support of a chief; failure, their disfavor. The ruling chief held some economic prerogatives. He owned larger orchards of breadfruit and coconut, received first fruits, and maintained centralized stores of breadfruit to support ceremonial feasts (especially chiefly life crisis events and cooperative labor) that chiefs might call. He funded the construction and owned the larger offshore canoes, which others had to ask special permission to borrow.

In addition to his own landholdings (which were more extensive than others), the ruling chief was considered the owner of his community's land—including the capital improvement of tree crops and irrigated fields. Although this gave him the right to first fruits, these productive facilities were held by the households that worked them. The ruling chief, however, endeavored to accumulate disposable surpluses and also encouraged others to be diligent and produce surpluses that supported ritual occasions.

AFRICAN CONTINENTAL CHIEFDOMS

Excellent ethnographies by social anthropologists documented African chiefdoms with a considerable scope of polity size. These societies accurately represented conditions that chiefdoms generally experienced in continental regions like Europe or North America, with much lower population densities than Polynesia and without intensive agriculture or irrigation.

Many Africans spoke closely related languages, suggesting fairly recent migrations similar to Pacific migrations. The Bantu linguistic group provides a good comparison with the variability observed among Polynesia chiefdoms. Bantu ancestors apparently were farmers in West Africa, perhaps in the tropical forest belt of southern Cameroon and Nigeria, although archaeological and genetic evidence is wanting. Based on linguistic evidence, they spread southward into the Congo forests, westward across the continent into the savanna country of East Africa, and southward into South Africa.

Unlike Polynesians, however, the rapid spread of Bantu people was into an occupied region. Foragers and pastoralists were widely distributed at low population densities so that the denser Bantu groups could replace them by exclusion and incorporation. Not all Bantu societies were regionally organized as chiefdoms but many developed regional polities. In contrast to the Polynesian examples, underlying segmentary principles suggests non-hierarchical Bantu organizational structures—as described by Roderick and Susan McIntosh.

Bantu subsistence was based heavily on agricultural cereal crops (especially millet) and animal herding, probably adopted from neighboring Nilotic groups in the eastern Africa savanna. The importance of animals in Old World chiefdoms across Eurasia and Africa contrasts sharply with New World chiefdoms with few domestic animals. Women provided the primary agricultural labor for households, such that polygynous marriages became a political strategy to increase surplus production and male status. Because animals were often used as bride wealth to obtain wives, success in animal husbandry was central to a man's political objectives. Considerable potential existed for intensification, especially with use of animal dung as landesque capital; but in drier environments water availability was challenging, and perhaps surprisingly irrigation was rarely practiced.

Warfare was characteristic of African chiefdoms. Young males raided for animals to use in bride wealth and establish status. Fighting existed over ownership of pastureland and conquest warfare was important in some of the chiefdom-states.

The Nuer

The basic organizing principle of the Bantu and other sub-Saharan groups was segmentary, meaning that groups formed and fractured according to contingent conditions at different social scales. In his classic ethnography of the Nilotic pastoralist Nuer without regional chiefdoms, E. E. Evans-Prichard captured the nature of African segmentary societies. A social segment fighting together held common kin-defined interests against a more distant faction. For example, a group of first cousins could unite to fight a group of second cousins over some insult, but both groups would unite to fight third cousins over the stealing of a cow. Fusing for common interest built larger groups, only to fission as their interests diverged.

The basic social and economic unit was the house, which in patriarchal cases typically included a man, his wives, and his children living within separate houses for each wife and enclosed by brush fencing. Homesteads contained families' herds and were placed adjacent to farmland. Houses were frequently isolated but could cluster in a small village often placed defensively on high ground. A village typically had common clan membership, although clans were also spread spatially across multiple villages. In forested regions Bantu clans could be matrilineal, but with significant herding in savannas, patrilineal structures appear to have become usual—perhaps linked to the importance of warriors to defend cattle and land.

Clans associated into tribes shared a common identity but inherently without stable internal political organization. Crosscutting the kin segments of African societies was the age-grade system, which subdivided males at three levels: the uncircumscribed (children), unmarried warriors, and married elders. Members of an age-grade were ceremonially circumcised together and held equivalent status. The grades were strongly hierarchical: children were associated with women, warriors fought to achieve status, and elders were respected leaders.

Warfare was prevalent in African societies and especially linked to herding (as seen among the Nuer). Because animals were movable wealth, they were easily stolen by raiders and required vigilant protection. Historically, slave raiding became widespread across Africa in response to demands of the world system. Male status was as a warrior with spear always in hand to protect kinsmen and cattle, and settlements were arranged defensively. War was both an organizing pressure and a means of fragmentation. In Africa regional polities of chiefdoms were based on conquest of lands and their people and the ability of would-be leaders to retain loyalty.

The Turu

Unlike Polynesia, nothing inherent in segmentary social structures creates hierarchy. The strongly decentralized structure of segmentary society is illustrated by Harold Schneider's description of the Bantu Turu of central Tanzania, East Africa. Their lack of regional hierarchy means that they should not be considered chiefdoms, but they represent the base from which chiefdoms formed.

The Turu were relatively high-density farmers (circa a hundred per square mile in the 1940s) growing millet and maize. Their basic unit was the polygynous homestead typified by Bantu societies. The household male was owner of farmland, animals, and other goods. Homesteads were regularly clustered into small villages of closely related homestead owners (typically brothers) who worked together for defense and farming. Surrounding shrub fences created private spaces and protected animals, stored grain, and women.

On pockets of better-watered soil, permanent farms were established and intensified with animal dung. Such landesque capital seems to have been linked to house ownership of land. Animals were the source of wealth for fertilizer and bride wealth payments for women, who in the polygynous families were the primary agricultural labor. Some economic inequality existed according to individuals striving to increase prestige, but such inequality did not translate into regionally centralized power. Cooperative labor and decision making took place within the homestead and village. Land held by individual houses could not be transferred outside of close kin, such as brothers in the village. Social groups remained small; although clans above the village were recognized, behaviorally they were of little significance.

The Turu illustrate how a segmentary society continually fissions economically and politically into constituent units. In contrast to many models of linkage between population density and political complexity, in Africa denser populations in societies like the Turu were significantly more decentralized than the chiefdoms of the Swazi. This was an outcome of the particular nature of the political economy, which created few opportunities for centralized control under this form of agricultural intensification without irrigation.

The Swazi

Because Bantu social organization was segmentary, the creation of regional chiefly polities among the Turu would seem to be inherently problematic, but it occurred again and again—perhaps surprisingly, especially in situations of relatively low population density. The regionally organized and hierarchically structured Bantu Swazi of eastern South Africa, described by Hilda Kuper in 1947, provides a good example of a super-complex chiefdom.

The Swazi were quite typical of Bantu segmentary societies. They were millet agriculturalists with wealth in animals. Historically, population densities were lower than for the Turu, perhaps only 30–40 per square mile. Focused on better-watered soils along streams, their shifting cultivation was less intensive. The settlement organization was much like the Turu—homestead units clustered into small villages with close kinship ties. Probably reflecting lower capital investment in fields, however, land was not owned by individual farmsteads but by corporate clans whose leaders allocated land in rotation to clan members. Kin groups worked together to prepare fields rapidly for planting; most agriculture was conducted by women at the household level. Warfare was common, both to defend and conquer lands and to raid for cattle. An African age-grade system defined Swazi warriors and elders, who served as community decision makers.

On top of this segmentary socioeconomic base was a regionally centralized and highly stratified state-like chiefdom with a subject population of perhaps 100,000. Their super-complex chiefdoms were analogous to the pastoralist "empires" that Nikolas Kradin describes for inner Asian aristocracies. The Swazi polity was tribal, representing a single ethnic group. The Swazi formed a large integrated polity by military displacement and conquest of land by Swazi paramounts; an obligation existed for the paramount to expand territory to support his group's growing population and competing interests.

In principle all land belonged to the paramount through right of conquest, but he distributed land to individual clans—creating a land-based system in which local chiefs were dependent on the paramount. Clans were ranked based on assertions of settlement priority; the first conquering clan had priority down to the most recent clan to acquire land. Clan chiefs held substantial independence and power in local affairs involving such matters as dispute settlement, emergency support, organizing cooperative labor crews, and running ceremonies. Cooperative labor and rituals were associated with feasts sponsored by these chiefs. Local chiefs, however, owed loyalty to their paramount, from whom all power derived.

This was a classic segmentary chiefdom in which power must be understood as multiscalar from the household to the large state-like chiefdom. The ruling clan stood above other clans; it claimed descent from a founding paramount and had a sovereign regency council with rights to surpluses derived from agriculture. The power structure of the paramount, however, was based more on a personalized chieftaincy network, the members of which resided in the paramount's villages. Regardless of clan affiliations, individuals could pledge loyalty to the paramount and be assigned a governing role according to status and ability.

The settlement system materialized the sociopolical structure of Swazi society. While the majority of the population lived in small village-hamlets clustered around their clan chief, central places existed. These were essentially simple hamlets but took on new functions of rule. Each new "king" established his own central place (capital) where he lived with multiple wives and the king mother. Here the high chiefs developed a ritual center with a shrine materializing his rule. Central storehouses and large corrals were well fortified to protect the leader's wealth, which supported his chiefly duties.

Through the paramount's reign the central settlement grew in size as the paramount assembled administrative specialists operating as governing administrators, but it never exceeded a few hundred residents. At his death the leader was buried at the central settlement, which formed a sequence maintained to support the line of rulers back to the ancestral home of the founding chiefs. The importance of warfare as a means to construct chiefdoms in relatively low-density segmentary societies is a theme addressed in Chapter 7.

SOUTHEAST ASIAN CHIEFDOMS

Throughout Southeast Asia states formed based on highly intensified irrigation, conquest warfare, elaborate ritual and religious centers, and extensive trade. These states, however, were quite patchy in their distributions and chiefdoms formed in interstitial highland areas, often positioned strategically to control trade critical to the states. In the hills of Burma, a series of historically closely related societies documented a spectrum of political forms from relatively egalitarian societies to agrarian states.

The primary ethnic division was between the Shan—a culture similar to southern Burmese irrigation-based states—and the Kachin, a diverse collection of hill people without irrigation. This spectrum was described by ethnographers and administrators of the British Empire, which dominated the region during the twentieth century. Edmund Leach's classic analysis of the region's political process stands out. Among related societies in Southeast Asia, Brian Hayden provides important ethnographic descriptions of the importance of feasting linked to prestige and power.

The Kachin

Highland Burma is a hilly tropical forested region in southern Asia between Thailand and India. Three major environmental and economic zones exist here. The lowlands along the major rivers are a human-engineered zone of dense Shan population dependent on irrigated rice that blanketed alluvial soils. Surrounding the valleys are the forested hills, where the Kachin groups lived. In the western hills, forests are well watered by annual monsoon rains.

Productive slash-and-burn agriculture by the Kachin produced dryland rice. A fairly long fallow cycle maintained soil fertility, and population densities were low and scattered in small villages or hamlets. Such settlements were relatively short term and people were not strongly tethered to place. In some locales, however, hill terraces were constructed to support permanent agricultural fields that allowed for higher densities and more permanent settlements. Long-distance trade, serving Chinese demand for special goods (especially jade), was important. Warfare was endemic, linked to revenge killing between local groups but also to controlling trade networks that supported emergent chiefdoms. To dominate trade, chiefs supported the construction of hill terraces to maintain permanent settlements at critical bottlenecks in commodity flows.

Leach described the Kachin sociopolitical system as one in constant flux, typical of segmentary societies but with strong elements of class structure not unlike what we have seen among the African Bantu. Among the Kachin he described the two modal systems of organization—his famous distinction between *gumsa* and *gumlao*. *Gumsa* can be taken as the foundational social organization; Leach called it anarchistic or democratic. Villages had chiefs who had little power beyond community ritual, such that community members had wide-ranging control over decision making. Since each village chief could claim to be equal to any other, no regional hierarchy or political system existed. The anarchistic Kachin contrasted sharply to the neighboring Shan in the river bottoms, who were organized by state-like feudal autocracies.

Gumlao was organizationally intermediary. Chiefs were able to extend power regionally by combined coercion and persuasion involving war, ritual feasting, supporting higher densities of people, and critically controlling both the agricultural terraces and the long-distance trade routes for moving wealth. Jonathan Friedman and Michael Rowlands describe this system as prestige goods exchanges—a particular form of political economy based on controlling distribution of wealth.

Political structures among the Kachin were inherently unstable, fluctuating between segmentation and hierarchy, democracy and autocracy, and anarchy and feudalism. The rise and fall of Kachin chiefdoms represented continuing processes involving economic control, warrior might, and ritual legitimation in feasting. Fluctuations in international wealth trade and broader international relationships created this constant flux. This was a key theme in the Caribbean maritime chiefdoms.

CIRCUM-CARIBBEAN CHIEFDOMS

On the Caribbean islands and fringing lowlands, chiefdoms existed broadly at the time of contact with the Spanish. Volume 4 of *The Handbook of South American Indians* distinguished Circum-Caribbean societies as intermediary in evolutionary complexity between the egalitarian tropical forest Amazonian tribes and the hierarchical Andean states. These societies became Kalervo Oberg's model to define chiefdoms as regional polities.

Although heavily impacted by western imperial expansion, historical accounts and archaeology can be linked to ethnographic descriptions. The cultural groups around the coastal regions and islands provide good examples of unstable complexity for Carib, Taino, and other ethnic groups. I focus here on Mary Helms's influential analysis of contact-period Panamanian chiefdoms, because of the importance long-distance relationships that are critical to understanding maritime chiefdoms (see Chapter 7).

Across the Caribbean an arc of islands provides rich agricultural soils and fishing opportunities that supported the evolution of chiefdoms, not unlike what has been observed for Polynesia. Fringing the sea are broad flats of savanna and mangroves that are fed by streams from the higher forested hills. Pockets of rich soils and good fishing created apparent abundance, which supported moderate population densities spread unevenly according to subsistence opportunities. With considerable local variation, the primary economy was agriculture—especially slash-and-burn cultivation (maize and root crops) with variable fallows, permanent tree crops (especially palm), and rich fishing in mangrove swamps, stream mouths, and open seas. Irrigation was limited to narrow streams coming out of the hills. Scattered hamlet-sized settlements varied greatly according to agricultural intensification along regularly flooded (and more fertile) riverbanks, but they were likely especially permanent near productive fishing areas.

Canoes were important both for fishing and travel between distant inlands, along coasts, and on rivers into the interior. Wild areas were quite important for hunting. Maritime mobility and navigational skill offered opportunities for trading and raiding. Except perhaps on the larger islands like Puerto Rico, agriculture, fishing, and hunting offered limited opportunities for chiefly control since people would easily move away to escape chiefly pressures. Warfare was apparently frequent; it was largely a matter of chiefs and critical to their attempts to expand political control and raiding.

Of particular interest is the Circum-Caribbean trade in wealth objects that involved gold from the coastal mountains of northern Colombia. By large canoes gold was traded east as far as Guyana and to the west along the Isthmus of Panama and into Costa Rica. Like the Kachin, long-distance movements of wealth appear to have been critical to emergent social complexity. Much of the variability in Circum-Caribbean chiefdoms reflected different possibilities to control agricultural land on the larger islands and flows of wealth on the coasts. Dramatically, Panamanian chiefdoms accumulated wealth in gold, obtained by trade with mining and manufacturing areas of Colombia.

Historical Chiefdoms of Panama

Focusing on well-documented historical chiefdoms of Panama, Helms describes the partition between chiefs and commoners. We know little from the historical documents about commoners, although we can suggest from modern ethnography that at the household level they were largely independent for subsistence. They would have made their own digging sticks, carrying baskets, nets, lines, canoes, and hunting equipment to exploit locally available resources.

Small hamlet-sized settlements were apparently fairly impermanent and scattered close to subsistence resources. Houses had thatched roofs and cane-and-plaster walls and were occupied by kin-based groups, probably with property rights in local resources and improved farmland. No discussion exists of larger commoner villages or of ceremonial architecture built within the commoner villages, although the modern Cuna descendants build large meetinghouses for public ceremonies and political debate. Settlements were undefended.

Chiefly status was inherited along a patrilineal senior line, similar to Polynesia. A high chief was born into rank and his success in war determined regional power. The chiefdom was forged by conquest and building a loyal chieftaincy. Although chiefs inherited status in the senior line, a commoner could be recognized as a low-ranked chief by service to a ruler. Chiefs were identified by distinctive dress and special adornments (including gold jewelry) and high chiefs were carried on litters. The ruling chief and his relatives lived in a central place among dispersed commoner settlements.

The political center was only as permanent as the chiefdom; it could include a large chiefly house, barracks for warriors, feasting space, a chiefly burial structure, and a storage complex for staples. Central settlements were surrounded by stone, wooden, or cactus walls and associated ditches, both defending stored wealth in people and objects and creating a distinctive social life. Residences thus materialized the power of the regional polity, maintaining (through force) rights to mobilize labor and productive agriculture. Slaves were those defeated in battle and may have provided labor to intensified agriculture—supporting the central settlements with warriors, administrators, and craftsmen. A large Panamanian chiefdom was said to have two thousand warriors, which might translate into a subject population in the low 10,000s spread across perhaps 50,000 square kilometers—based on the historical separation of major centers.

Helms's central argument emphasizes the importance of long-distance relationships to make and maintain the ruling chief's distinction. Redundant and largely unimproved agriculture and other resources offered little opportunity for power and control. Rather, central settlements were placed to control access to metal flows from Colombia along the eastern coast and into the interior. Gold and other objects from afar had inherent distinctiveness in material qualities of brilliance, able to be crafted into figured objects with symbolic significance.

Figure 1.4 shows a frog pendant that was cast in gold using the complicated lost-wax method. Such technical sophistication evidently involved manufacture by gifted craftsmen. To the degree that access to these objects could be controlled by chiefs, they could express magical-religious powers and warrior strength. (The frog, for example, was a symbol of rain and agricultural

Figure 1.4. Golden frog pendant, a wealth object from Panamanian chiefdoms. The metal was traded, presumably by boat, from northern Colombia, and crafted by a highly skilled metallurgist probably attached to a chief. The Metropolitan Museum of Art, Michael C. Rockefeller Memorial Collection, Bequest of Nelson A. Rockefeller, 1979 (1979.206.1350).

fertility.) Probably ownership of canoes by chiefs supported distant travels. By controlling foreign wealth, chiefs could express special magical powers of a shaman.

THE BOTTOM LINE

Ethnographic and historical cases of chiefdoms help define the political character of intermediate-level societies that denote the broad category of chiefdoms. They give a sense of variability with a rather typical political process to centralized power. Chiefdoms vary greatly in population densities, environmental possibilities, subsistence economies, and technologies. Although not elaborated in the brief ethnographic summaries, the historical distinctions of each cultural group are profound. Specifics of kinship, community structure, religion, myths, and much more can only be understood in terms of culture histories.

Within a single cultural area, however, societies develop into political spectra from egalitarian communities through state-like paramouncies. What all the cases have in common is the political drive toward developing regional institutions based on the accumulation of power through manipulating economic, warrior, and religious activities. I discuss these alternative sources of power in Chapter 2.

Although constructed differently based on the specificity of each chiefdom, chiefs always formulate power strategies to rise to preeminence. At the same time, interests involving families and their communities act to limit or coopt political consolidation. The evolutionary dynamics responsible for regional political institutions in chiefdoms should be considered as a mediator between top-down (chiefly) and bottom-up (community) interests and balance of power. The attempt to identify chiefdoms as a particular evolutionary type in a stair-wise evolutionary progression is incorrect, but changing political economies in varying forms characterize all societies organized between the village-level autonomy of anarchistic societies and the formal superstructure of states.

ADDITIONAL READINGS

Discussions of Theories Related to Chiefdoms

Carneiro, Robert L., Leonid Grinin, and Andrey Korotayev (editors). 2017. *Chiefdoms: Yesterday and Today*. Clinton Corners, NY: Eliot Werner Publications. This book provides up-to-date discussions of chiefdoms, including a lengthy chapter by Robert Carneiro emphasizing the importance of warfare and refuting Norman Yoffee's criticism of the chiefdom concept. Blair Gibson considers the organizational scale of chiefdom confederacies. Russian scholars provide good overviews of social evolution and chiefdoms.

Earle, Timothy. 1987. Chiefdoms in Archaeological and Ethnohistorical Perspective. *Annual Review of Anthropology* 16:279–308. Review article summarizing the use of chiefdom concepts in anthropology and archaeology.

Flannery, Kent V., and Joyce Marcus. 2012. *The Creation of Inequality: How Our Prehistoric Ancestors Set the State for Monarchy, Slavery, and Empire.* Cambridge, MA: Harvard University Press. Brings together ethnographies and archaeology looking at the transitional role of chiefdoms in emergent social and political inequality. This is a classic study of archaeology as a historical science capable of looking at problems of social relevance.

Friedman, Jonathan, and Michael J. Rowlands. 1977. Notes Towards an Epigenetic Model of the Evolution of "Civilisation." In *The Evolution of Social Systems*, edited by Jonathan Friedman and Michael J. Rowlands, pp. 201–276. London: Duckworth. Chapter models prestige goods economies, an important concept in the study of many chiefdoms. Prestige economies represent wealth finance as an exclusionary strategy.

Hayden, Brian. 2016. *Feasting in Southeast Asia.* Honolulu: University of Hawaii Press. Looks ethnographically at the role of feasting by aggrandizers in the emergence of social stratification involving chiefdoms.

Detailing Variability in Chiefdoms

Drennan, Robert D., and Carlos A. Uribe (editors). 1987. *Chiefdoms in the Americas.* Lanham, MD: University Press of America. Collection of chapters documenting variations among American chiefdoms, including an important chapter by Drennan describing how chiefdoms can be studied archaeologically by population distribution within settlement hierarchies. He has continued to work on quantitative approaches to chiefdoms, looking at major variability across cases.

Earle, Timothy (editor). 1991. *Chiefdoms: Power, Economy, and Ideology.* Cambridge, UK: Cambridge University Press. Based on a School of American Research Advanced Seminar on variation in chiefdoms. This book brings together leading scholars considering chiefdoms including Gary Feinman, Antonio Gilman, Patrick Kirch, and Kristian Kristiansen.

Feinman, Gary M., and Jill Neitzel. 1984. Too Many Types: An Overview of Sedentary Prestate Societies in the Americas. *Advances in Archaeological Method and Theory* 7:39–102. Using a systematic analysis of ethnographically described chiefdoms from the Human Relations Area Files, this article looks at variations among chiefdoms, showing that chiefdoms cannot be seen as a societal type identified by a specific list of traits.

McIntosh, Susan Keech (editor). 1999. *Beyond Chiefdoms: Pathways to Complexity in Africa*. New York: Cambridge University Press. This book looks at segmentary societies in Africa that do not have strong social hierarchies and centralized leadership. The editor wishes to move "beyond" the classical definition of chiefdoms (as described by Elman Service) to understand a much less centralized form of regional societies found in Africa.

Redmond, Elsa M. (editor). 1998. *Chiefdoms and Chieftaincies in the Americas*. Gainesville, FL: University Press of Florida. Looks at variations in the degree of centrality among chiefdoms of the Americas by bringing together cases of New World chiefdoms.

Ethnographies of Chiefdoms

These ethnographies illustrate tribal societies operating under different economic conditions and contrasting patterns of institutional scale and hierarchy.

Bloch, Marc. 1964. *Feudal Society*. 2 vols. Chicago: University of Chicago Press. Looks at feudal Europe, discussing political and economic organization that ranged from chiefdoms to state societies. Especially important is its understanding of stratified—but relatively weakly centralized—political systems base on land ownership of noble estates.

Evans-Prichard, E. E. 1940. *The Nuer: A Description of the Modes of Livelihood and Political Institutions of a Nilotic People*. Oxford, UK: Oxford University Press. Classic British ethnography of a segmentary African society with weak chiefs managing a fusion-fission model of social formation.

Firth, Raymond. 1936. *We the Tikopia: A Sociological Study of Kinship in Primitive Polynesia*. London: George Allen & Unwin. Classic British ethnography of a small-scale Polynesian chiefdom with weak chiefs involved primarily in ritual, in contrast to the Marquesas and the Hawaiian Island chiefdoms.

Handy, E. S. Craighill. 1923. *The Native Culture in the Marquesas*. Bulletin No. 79. Honolulu: Berniece P. Bishop Museum. Ethnography of Marquesan chiefdoms by an American anthropologist. The Bishop Museum Bulletin published primary descriptions of the Pacific Island groups, which represented a full spectrum of chiefdoms.

Helms, Mary W. 1976. *Ancient Panama: Chiefs in Search of Power*. Austin: University of Texas Press. A classic ethnohistorical study of power dependent on distant chiefly relationships. Good ethnographies are also available on the contemporaneous Kuna, who have effectively resisted full incorporation by the Panamanian state.

Junker, Laura Lee. 1999. *Raiding, Trading, and Feasting: The Political Economy of Philippine Chiefdoms*. Honolulu: University of Hawaii Press. Chiefdoms developed in the Philippines, where they controlled international trade by merchants handling commodities desired by the Chinese.

Kuper, Hilda. 1947. *An African Aristocracy: Rank Among the Swazi*. Oxford, UK: Oxford University Press. A student of Malinowski describes a Bantu "kingdom" in South Africa. This complex chiefdom was based on conquest warfare.

Leach, Edmund. 1965. *Political Systems of Highland Burma: A Study of Kachin Social Structure*. Boston: Beacon Press. Leach provides a historical and ethnographic description of traditional tribal society describing highly dynamic political arrangements based on changing economic conditions. Emphasis is on process rather than structure, critiquing British structuralism. Friedman and Rowlands's model of prestige goods exchanged is based on this important study.

Sahlins, Marshall. 1958. *Social Stratification in Polynesia*. Seattle: University of Washington Press. Classic study of adaptive radiation in historically related chiefly societies based on different ecological and economic conditions. The scale of integration and social stratification represents a full spectrum of chiefdoms.

Schneider, Harold. 1964. A Model of African Indigenous Economy and Society. *Comparative Studies in Society and History* 7:35–55. An economic anthropologist describes a relatively high-density Bantu society illustrating household independence and resistance to social hierarchy. Provides an important contrast to Kuper's ethnography of the Swazi kingdom.

CHAPTER 2

EVOLUTIONARY THEORY INTEGRATING ANTHROPOLOGY

From anthropology's beginning evolution has been a central theme of integration and division in our discipline. To understand the meaning and use of chiefdom, we must understand its role in and critique of sociocultural evolution. I start by describing the broader context of evolutionary theory as it transformed intellectual thinking at anthropology's foundation. In *Origin of Species*, Charles Darwin inspired natural and social scientists to rethink the history of Anthropos: human origins, languages, societies, politics, and religions. Evolution became an integrating premise defining anthropology.

EVOLUTION

Evolution is a very broad concept involving systematic change in various spheres—from planetary physics, geology, and biology to human social organization and culture. Evolution is not a monolithic phenomenon but represents processes channeling predictable change in diverse natural systems. Some evolutionary processes may be closely linked, while others are system-specific; the degree of similarities is an empirical question. Traits that help define evolution are history, process, and selection.

Evolution looks at processes of selection ("biased transmission") that channels changes. Ernest Mayr, the great evolutionary biologist, described evolution as a historical science. Selection directs biological change; it does not create novelty. Evolution is descent with modification, and unlike some earlier conceptions evolution is not predetermined to create specific forms or directions. It should not be seen as goal seeking—for example, as inevitable progress toward human perfectibility, democracy, or the like. Selective processes differ according to the phenomena under consideration but they involve sequential, systematic change following patterns that create diverse forms.

Emerging Ideas of Evolution

During the nineteenth century, publications by Darwin, Charles Lyell, Karl Marx, Herbert Spencer, and others outlined how geology, biology, and society can be understood in terms of change channeled by uniform processes. Largely gone was a sense of a static world, created by God and changing only episodically according to human will and divine purpose. Rather, to understand systematic change and resulting variability requires a scientific understanding of the uniform forces that shape historical formations. Evolution is the process of diversification.

Although social evolution is key to understanding the long history of human cultures, many anthropologists have questioned its use—partly on empirical grounds, but more broadly because of its potential abuses. Evolutionary thinking has been used to justify western claims to superiority and colonial expansion, infamously exemplified by German anthropology during the Nazi era and by British and French colonial policy. Although a history of racist politics continues to haunt anthropology, evolutionary studies refute racist fallacies. Humans are undeniably animals, one species, and our biological evolutionary history is evident.

From the sixteenth to nineteenth centuries, Europeans lived in times of deep religious beliefs, but also of discovery. European nations were expanding as never before—exploring, connecting, and colonizing the world. Europeans encountered a startling new diversity of plants, animals, and people unlike anything they had known before. They became fascinated with the exotic, building museums of natural history to warehouse, analyze, and understand the world's diversity.

To explain this diversity became a search for God's plan. For example, Carl Linnaeus—a Swedish scholar and naturalist born in 1707—sought to categorize the world's diversity of plant and animal kingdoms. As an ardent Christian, he believed that the living world would document God's plan. What Linnaeus described was a system of inclusion based on degrees of embedded similarities described as species, genera (closely similar species), families (clusters of genera), and so on up to the kingdoms of plants and animals.

The biblical story told of the creation of humans in God's image. But all humans did not look alike. They had visually distinctive characteristics of skin color, facial features, hair, and height, and these differences were reinforced by different behaviors like dress and body treatment. These dissimilarities seemed to justify a general (although not uncontested) view that "racial" differences were based on multiple creations—some thought to be superior, others inferior and perhaps even not human at all. Such ideas were convenient to justify behaviors including extermination of competing groups, colonial conquest and domination, and of course slavery.

But at the same time geologists started to understand geological processes (uniformitarianism) such as erosion and deposition that slowly crafted disparate landforms. To understand uniform processes seemed to require deep historical knowledge of eons of time, well beyond the biblical sequence of a few thousand years. Associated with different rock strata, sequences of plant and animal fossils included species that no longer existed and others that seemed to replace each other through geological strata. Although Linnaeus's system of classification proved sufficiently robust to describe living and extinct plants and animals, the degrees of similarities and differences that he recognized seem to suggest a history of change shaped like the branches of a tree. God's plan appeared to include continuity and change across vast time scales.

With prominent scientists such as Harvard geologist Louis Agassiz remaining committed to creationism, Charles Darwin overcame a conceptual obstacle to formulate biological evolutionary theory. Darwin identified natural selection as the uniform mechanism for change. Descent with modification was channeled in particular circumstances by variable reproductive success. A clear understanding of the contexts in which selection takes place is critical to evolution. With many additions and modifications, biological evolution—the Darwinian synthesis—is foundational to all biological sciences.

Evolution, Anthropology, and Racism

Evolutionary biology became integral to the new field of anthropology. Although originally a hypothesis that humans, apes, and monkeys had common ancestors, biological anthropology has gradually documented the fossil evidence for human divergence from the primate family. Genetic similarities between chimpanzees and humans now suggest that we are of the same genus. We are *Homo sapiens*, the chimpanzees are *Homo troglodytes*, and the bonobos are *Homo paniscus*. The three species are biological cousins but with remarkable differences, some biological but others clearly representing extraordinary changes documented by human cultures.

Which brings us back to race, a categorization of humans that is broadly believed around the world. The real problem appears to be lingering elements of creationism—humans are superior to animals and some are more superior than others. This is a false and highly politicized application of evolutionary theory, but one that served conveniently to explain domination and exclusion. To cleanse itself should anthropology jettison biological and sociocultural evolution? I argue that understanding the deep historical processes of human diversity as both biological and cultural should be central to our discipline.

NINETEENTH CENTURY SOCIOCULTURAL EVOLUTION

Sociocultural evolution helps us understand historically systematic change involving various selective processes. For societies and culture, selection happens at multiple levels that can be simplified as bottom-up processes by which individuals and small groups make behavior choices—especially regarding subsistence and social affiliations (relationships) and top-down intergroup processes involving power relationships used by groups in competition and dominance. Individuals choose certain practices and technologies because of their effectiveness and groups expand or contract based on power relations.

In Europe, Darwin's theory—coupled with industrial growth—seemed to make evolutionary schemes incorporating progress an evident means to understand human societal differences. Western advances in ship technology, steam power, and new weaponry created fast transportation, industrial production, and overwhelming military might that seemed to justify ideas of western superiority. A sense of stasis was replaced by progress and a manifest destiny for the West to dominate the rest.

Such ideas were easily and unfortunately linked to evolutionary thinking. As knowledge of non-western cultures increased, social scientists began amassing and attempting to explain the diversity in human societies. This new knowledge seemed to fit perceived notions of western superiority, but eventually those simplifying assumptions were challenged within anthropology.

Herbert Spencer

After reading Darwin, Herbert Spencer coined the phrase "survival of the fittest" to capture societal replacements. He argued that societies followed pathways of change that could be understood by natural laws. Accumulated knowledge allowed technologically advanced societies to replace more primitive ones. As shown by colonial expansion, it was evident to westerners that they must be smarter and harder-working people, prospering over the dull and lazy peoples trapped in traditional ways. Racism lay close to an idea that western virtues of hard work and creativity were destined to dominate the world. Such ideas (referred to as Social Darwinism) were popular with the public and fit conveniently with ethnocentric mindsets of manifest destiny for Euro-American people to lead the world.

In the nineteenth century, evolutionism was basic to new museums of natural history—home to professional curators from geology, botany, and zoology. Coming into the museums were also cultural collections from the traditional peoples of Asia, Africa, the Pacific, and the Americas. Based on assumptions of technological progress linked to Spencer's writing, these new cultural collections were classified as cultural types arranged along "evolutionary" scales from most primitive (Stone Age gatherers) to most complex (European industrial states, of course). Archaeologists in Europe were already organizing prehistoric collections as a technology-based, three-stage system—Stone, Bronze, and Iron ages.

Morgan, Marx, and Engels

At this time anthropologists were armchair intellectuals with limited personal experience outside Europe. They depended on missionaries, colonial administrators, and travelers for their information. Lewis Henry Morgan's *Ancient Society* became foundational to the new field of anthropology and social evolution was his organizing theme. He amassed knowledge of contemporary world cultures and proposed a pseudo-historical classification to order them: lower and upper savagery, lower and upper barbarism, and finally civilization.

The original humans, "in a state of nature," were thought similar to modern hunter-gatherers, foraging for what nature offered. Life was considered to have been hard. With the invention of agriculture, however, people could settle down, making life easier and allowing developments of sophisticated knowledge and social relationships. As technology advanced and people became increasingly specialized, civilizations emerged that allowed people to free themselves from constant drudgery and create religion and fine arts. Fundamental to this evolutionary scheme were improvements in culture requiring more sophisticated ideas and technology. Achievements of modern European civilization represented a crowning glory.

Morgan's overview of human societies guided the understanding of Karl Marx and Friedrich Engels, who formulated a theory of social evolution based on historical materialism. Marx and Engels looked at different degrees of social and political inequality linked historically to modes of production. Modes combined factors of technology (means of production) and social formations (relations of production). In simple terms, technology created particular economic conditions—like scale and complexity of textile production—in which different social classes could benefit differentially. Capitalists owned the textile factories from which they derived profits and workers received wages for their labor.

Classes benefited differently because of their social relationship to the economy. Using historical cases—Germanic, Slavonic, Asiatic, feudal, and capitalist—Marx and Engels conceived of a typology of modes of production in human history resulting in advances, setbacks, and a glorious revolutionary future. These were partially arranged sequentially, according to technological and social process, leading to utopian communism. In his eulogy at Marx's funeral, Engels affirmed, "Just as Darwin discovered the law of development of organic nature, so Marx discovered the law of development of human history" (1883). The selective mechanism identified by Marx was the top-down assertion of powerful classes to control productive forces used for political domination.

Spencer versus Marx: Foundations of Social Evolutionary Thought

Increasing knowledge of world cultures became understood by the two evolutionary formulations articulated by Spencer and Marx. Based on the experiences of the Industrial Revolution, both assumed (contra Darwin) that evolution was progressive. Spencer saw the result of evolution as European civilization. Marx, rather, saw the inequalities of European capitalism and the possibility to create a new world order. Both had little direct interest in bottom-up processes, although Spencer's work included race-based assumptions of higher intelligence/cultural advantages of the West and Marx hoped to mobilize workers of the world to throw off capitalism.

Top-down selection was critical to both approaches but at different social levels. Spencer emphasized that whole societies could expand to exclude more "primitive" societies because of cultural advantages. Marx emphasized selection based on the relative power of classes linked to economic position. Logically, chiefdoms—like regional polities—would have emerged as precursors to states and civilization.

TWENTIETH CENTURY AMERICAN RELATIVISM AS A HISTORICAL SCIENCE

In the twentieth century, expanding professional knowledge of non-western societies resulted in a fundamental rethinking of evolutionary process. Most importantly, the race-based assumptions of evolution as relentless progress were increasingly questioned by anthropology. Non-western societies were to be appreciated, if not gloried. Based on a misplaced notion of progress, the theoretical formulations of Spencer and Marx came to be questioned within academia, especially since these ideas had been co-opted to justify unimaginable offenses against humanity.

Nineteenth century theories were seen as wrong on two counts: human races were highly variable internally with no differentiation by intelligence or other capabilities, and human societies showed no ranking of overall life quality. As emphasized by biologists, evolution as a theoretical process is *not* progress; it is change with modification. I argue that evolution as an explanation for diversity and change has remained fundamental to anthropology, but it must be stripped of its misuses.

The true horror of racism justified by evolutionary thinking became obvious with fascist genocide. Wanting to create a master race, Nazis adopted the selection theory used by stockbreeders to apply to humans. During the early 1900s, eugenics sought to identify humans who were judged undesirable for sterilization. Nazis latched on to this idea, first sterilizing and then killing those with epilepsy, Down syndrome, and the like. Bent on a nationalist (Aryan) agenda, fascists scaled up their selection into industrial killings of

Jews, the Roma, and other "undesirables" (homosexuals, Communists). This horrendous use of an evolutionary argument, although never part of evolutionary theory, caused a broad disciplinary rejection of nineteenth century evolutionary thinking.

For brevity, in the following summary I focus on a few individuals to illustrate broad trends. This narrative, however, necessarily deemphasizes many contributions. I largely bypass ideas of prominent scholars—including, for example, Robert Boyd, Robert Dunnell, Ian Hodder, and Leslie White—all of whom contributed in differing ways to understanding sociocultural evolution.

Franz Boas

To understand the role of ethnography in evolutionary studies, we start with Franz Boas, who became the chief critic of nineteenth century evolutionary approaches and the major spokesperson for appreciating cultural differences. Trained in (and bored by) physical sciences of light, Boas accompanied a German expedition to Baffin Island in the Canadian arctic in 1883. Perhaps to find himself, Boas stayed for a year to observe Inuit foragers. He identified with their ingenuity, creativity, and sophistication; they lived with extraordinary ecological challenges to craft a meaningful cultural world. His appreciation of traditional people was at the root of future American ethnography. No evolutionary scheme to categorize cultures as more or less advanced could explain away the richness of their lifeways and histories.

Boas sought to explain broadly unrecognized values of diverse cultures. His main contribution was cultural relativism; all cultures had equally long histories and cultural qualities that must be understood on their own terms. He trained a generation of dominant American anthropologists including Ruth Benedict, Melville Herskovits, Alfred Kroeber, and Margret Mead. Under their influence American anthropology assumed a mission to make cultural and biological differences safe from a world propelled by nationalism, genocide, and racial hatred.

Boas and his proteges considered themselves empirical scientists, describing cultures by participant observation and systematic interviews. They criticized early evolutionary syntheses as based on poor evidence without historical documentation. Ordering societies in terms of modern characteristics was ultimately Eurocentric. Working especially in the Americas, they conducted detailed ethnographic studies to document cultural traits—formulating strategies for interviewing especially elderly native speakers who retained detailed traditional knowledge. For each culture they created a trait list including house types, subsistence practices, marriage rules, moccasin forms, and the like that described cultures as they saw them.

A broader appreciation of non-western cultures was encouraged by presenting world cultures to the public in natural history museum exhibitions, popular general books on the nature of culture, and detailed ethnographies (e.g, describing the "penny capitalism" of Maya marketplaces). Collected by Boas from indigeous people of America's Northwest Coast for the 1893 Chicago's World Fair, the wood carvings of house posts (totem poles) and fantastic masks showed traditional creativity and interest. They can still be seen at the Field Museum in Chicago.

Figure 2.1 shows a Kwakwaka'wakw (Kwakiutl) transformational mask. In elaborate ceremonies such masks were worn to create dramatic visual effects, showing shamanistic abilities to transform into animals. The high quality of such a mask portrayed the elevated status and magical power of the hosting chief. Masks and other ceremonial objects were made especially for chiefs by skilled craftsmen.

Figure 2.1. Kwakiutl transformation mask carved by Bob Harris (Xi'xa'niyus). Collected for the 1893 Chicago International Exhibit by George Hunt working with Franz Boas. © The Field Museum, Image #A108351c, Cat. #19166, photographer Ron Testa.

Boas and American anthropologists rejected nineteenth century evolutionary thinking. Analyzing cultural distribution of traits according to degrees of similarities and differences was not unlike Linneaus's famous biological taxonomies. In his attack on cultural evolution, Robert Lowie described culture as a "thing of shreds and patches," a random assemblage of traits, each with its own history (1920, p. 441). Cultural patterns were interpreted as the result of innovations and diffusion. But how did they explain the assembling of traits into a cultural package? Some selective processes must have been involved and general concepts of diffusion and acculturation were the foundation.

Under Boas's influence American anthropology embraced archaeology to document histories of traits—their origins, spread, and assembly as distinctive archaeological cultures. Cultural traditions studied by archaeology were assemblages of diagnostic artifact styles for pottery, lithics, housing, and burial practices. Archaeology provided the hard data of temporary change in cultural traits on which American anthropology had come to rely. This connection between cultural anthropology and archaeology became foundational to twentieth century American anthropology.

The historical science of Boas emphasized detailed description of cultural difference freed from biases of primitiveness. In line with biological evolution, it was based on empiricism and rejected assumptions of progressive change. Rather than natural selection, however, it identified unspecified mechanisms of cultural selection by innovation and diffusion. Humans were seen as inventive and inquisitive in creating their own cultures. Boas freed anthropology from inherent ethnocentrism of the previous "evolutionary" formulations, but was this really a rejection of evolutionary theory? Probably Boas thought it was because of the insidious uses to which evolutionary concepts had seen service. My view, however, is that Boasian anthropology was fundamentally evolutionary (systematic change in traits) and a means to study cultural differences, and that archaeology provides the real historical evidence. An understanding of cultural selection, however, remained imprecise.

TWENTIETH CENTURY BRITISH STRUCTURAL FUNCTIONALISM AS A HISTORICAL SCIENCE

By midcentury British anthropology provided a new selective mechanism to understand human societies. It was called structural functionalism (or simply functionalism for short), a science-based endeavor developing the approach of French sociologist Emile Durkheim. The premise was that all institutions—such as religious practices, political organizations, and economies—functioned to maintain a society by providing structures for action. Structural functionalism dominated British anthropology with famous scholars including E. E. Evans-Pritchard, Raymond Firth, Bronisław

Malinowski, and A. R. Radcliffe-Brown. Committed to empiricism, they traveled to the British colonies to document and understand traditional, non-modern societies. The result was a library of influential ethnographies, several of which provided basic descriptions of chiefdoms (see Chapter 1).

One of the first scholars to incorporate functionalism into American anthropology was the economic historian Karl Polanyi. He created the school of substantivist economics, meaning that economic flows met a society's material needs and desires. The economy as an institution functioned to form and maintain social structure by a formal (instituted) mechanism of distribution. Different organizing principles were thus appropriate to support a particular structural form—reciprocity in villages, redistribution in chiefdoms and archaic states, and market exchange in capitalist states. The concept of redistribution as an economic mechanism became basic for understanding chiefdoms.

British functionalists criticized evolutionary approaches of the nineteenth century as wild extrapolations based on assertions that contemporary, less complex societies offered surrogates for ancient social formations. Radcliffe-Brown asserted that societies studied by anthropologists were without histories and he attacked Boas and American anthropology as creating pseudo-science, because no historical data existed to study actual change. What a mistake.

British functionalism's radical anti-evolutionary stance was based on an ignorance (or perhaps dismissal) of the historical evidence that archaeology could provide. In Britain and throughout Europe, cultural anthropology and archaeology were—and still are—housed in separate academic disciplines, and only in the United States (under the influence of Boas) was a historical anthropology seen as foundational. At midcentury, however, Radcliffe-Brown was probably correct that historical approaches were limited by relatively poor data, because archaeology was still a nascent thing. This immaturity of archaeology, however, was to change dramatically as the century moved on.

CULTURAL ECOLOGY AND FUNCTIONALISM

Structural functionalism was introduced into America during World War II when Malinowski and other scholars came to the United States. Its attractiveness was an ability to make sense of how and why cultures had internal coherence—why cultures were particular assemblages of traits. The concept of cultures as traits continued to be important in America but a new interest focused on organizations. Functionalism added the selective mechanism for cultural change and diversification; traits would be invented, diffused, and accepted according to functionality for the cultural whole. Adopting functional selection, American anthropology created a new evolutionary synthesis.

White and Steward

The reconfiguring of American anthropology had two leading ethnographers—Leslie White at the University of Michigan and Julian Steward at Columbia University and the University of Illinois. As I read their work, both White and Steward were dedicated non-doctrinaire Marxists but with distinctive approaches. White argued that worldwide technological advances increased energy capture (labor power harnessed to fire, animal, water, and wind) and created progressively increasing social complexity. Although his writing inspired materialist explanations, White's approach lacked a plausible selective mechanism to explain variation.

Julian Steward, by contrast, adopted a functionalism (which he called cultural ecology) that integrated seamlessly within the Boasian approach of his training. From a bottom-up perspective, he understood how individuals and groups make choices about technologies, organizations, and beliefs that allow them to survive under changing environmental conditions. These choices, however, were made within a cultural context of appropriateness with traditional practices. This was the underlying appreciation that Boas originally showed for the Artic Inuit people.

Steward called the adaptive assemblage of traits a cultural core, defined as "the constellation of features which are most closely related to subsistence activities and economic arrangements" (1955, p. 37). Although many cultural traits could be seen as but shreds and patches of group histories, core traits were basic to social survival, and similar cultural core configurations could be expected cross-culturally as social groups adapted to similar conditions. Among high-density agriculturalists, for example, Steward and Karl Wittfogel suggested that administrative state management developed independently around the world because of similar conditions (dry environments made fruitful with irrigation). Variation in culture cores corresponded closely with Marx's modes of production.

Steward's seminal study of Shoshone foragers in the American Great Basin documented how the social formation of low-density foragers in an arid landscape changed seasonally in response to shifting subsistence opportunities. Bands would disperse as individual families scattered to harvest seeds at one season, only to coalesce at another to hunt rabbits cooperatively. He developed his settlement pattern approach to study variable seasonal and social activities of human groups in representing different locations of habitation and activity. Steward envisioned such adaptations as outcomes of cultural evolution, creating multilinear evolution—driven by selective value of core traits depending on specific historical, technological, and environmental circumstances that would show common patterns cross-culturally.

Steward encouraged archaeologists to look at patterns of change from this cultural ecology perspective. Perhaps the most important outcome was the widespread adoption of settlement pattern studies in American archaeology.

Steward organized the groundbreaking Virú Valley Project on coastal Peru, which looked both ethnographically and archaeologically at changing settlement patterns there. His approach was closely compatible with historical materialism, although the explicit connection of his work to Marxism waited to be elaborated by his students Morton Fried and Eric Wolf.

In 1955 Steward introduced the idea that cultures are organized by "levels of sociocultural integration" (family, local community, regional polity, and super-regional state). A primary research object of cultural ecology became to identify the factors that made new levels of integration advantageous. Like the Darwinian synthesis in biology, societal change was without goals, except to select new adaptive traits to deal with existing and emergent challenges—but trends could still exist in population growth and technological intensification. Social institutions were viewed by Steward as technologies of everyday life, and thus cultural evolution was a multilinear process selecting cultural traits appropriate to contrasting environments and technologies.

Steward's Intellectual Successors

Making use of anthropology's growing ethnographic corpus, Morton Fried and Elman Service—with Steward at Columbia—formulated typologies of social types that shaped much anthropological thinking into the 1960s and seventies. They specified differences in societal scale and identified key selective mechanisms for change. Service formulated the prevailing typology: *band–tribe–chiefdom–state*. Each type represented an increasing scale of integration.

Service adopted Polanyi's association of economic mechanisms with social types. Using a functionalist logic, he discussed how new levels of integration helped groups solve problems associated with population growth and agricultural intensification. The regional hierarchy of chiefs resolved disputes, coordinated labor organization (as involved irrigation), and redistributed specialized local economies.

Service's scheme was an attractive functionalist understanding of how cultural traits had been invented and diffused by groups as a means of survival. His typology became the standard scheme used by students and professionals alike to classify societies into scales of organization and to explain why groups developed new social organizations for utilitarian reasons. Following Steward the chiefdom type provided an intermediate-scale assortment of societies with a regional organization. Despite subsequent criticism, his scheme was neither unilinear nor irreversible. It represented societal formations based on selective advantage to both individuals and groups.

In Steward's conception new economic formations were developed as new levels of social integration were created. In all societies—from simple foragers to agrarian states—the family was the basic subsistence unit. Each household sought self-sufficiency by having access to needed subsistence resources and maintaining labor for required tasks. These family units became embedded by reciprocal relations within a community scale to solve problems for which households had insufficient labor, and these communities became embedded in chiefdoms organized by redistribution. Multiscalar societies were thus built up from their constituent parts, each continuing to maintain its own strategic organizational objectives. As discussed in Chapter 1, the multiscalar character of human society is essential for understanding chiefdoms.

Substantivist economics studied the function of economies to build and maintain social institutions. Marshal Sahlins's influential book *Stone Age Economics* showed how redistribution in Polynesia supported the central position and prestige of chiefs as guarantors of economic well-being. He also recognized that economies functioned at multiple levels for the household, the community, and the regional polity.

Problems with Models of Social Evolution Based on Ethnography

Based on variation in ethnographic groups, cultural anthropologists formed typologies of social levels of integration in which chiefdoms represented an intermediate scale. The selective mechanisms identified were largely functional with some consideration of power. Two problems were evident. First, the typologies appeared to be intellectually similar to nineteenth century evolutionary schemes rating societies from simple to complex. Second, both were pseudo-historical and relied on an evolutionary logic to order contemporaneous cases into a purported sequence.

Details from the ethnographic record were seductive as the means to identify mechanisms of change, but only historical change could test these hypotheses. Here was the value of American anthropology, where ethnography and archaeology could unite within the discipline of anthropology. Anthropological archaeology has progressively taken on the role of documenting and testing theories of social evolution. Influenced especially by Steward, archaeology developed a distinctive processual approach to social evolution combining cultural ecology (bottom-up) and political economy (top-down).

FUNCTIONALISM AND THE NEW ARCHAEOLOGY

To understand archaeology's role in studying social evolution, I concentrate on American archaeology during the second half of the twentieth century. Although prefigured by V. Gordon Childe's processual framework in Eurasia, the ethnographic work of Sahlins, Service, Steward, and Wolf proved to be most inspiring. Improvements in the sophistication of archaeological research were partly theoretical but heavily methodological, incorporating important advances in settlement pattern studies, dating, chemical characterization, and computer analyses of large data sets.

Cultural Ecology and Archaeology

Steward's cultural ecology was instrumental for reintroducing explicit concern with social evolution into archaeology. In 1946 Peru's Virú Valley Project supported Gordon Willey's application of a cultural ecology study in archaeology. His monograph *Settlement Patterns in the Virú Valley* established a new standard for regional archaeological investigations, which moved the field away from simple cultural trait lists toward an understanding of cultural systems as means of adaptation.

Willey looked at changing economies in terms of site associations with different resources, documented the intensification of agriculture with irrigation systems, and suggested the evolution of social complexity as a result of growing population. Settlement pattern changes showed emergent settlement hierarchies articulated with urbanism, large cemeteries, and specialized ceremonial centers. Using settlement patterns, American archaeologists began studying regional social systems as dynamic long-term adaptations to specific environments with innovation and adoption of new technologies, including the formation of regional social organizations such as chiefdoms and states.

The next generation of archaeologists followed Steward's logic to try to discover the prime movers of social evolution. Possible prime movers included population growth, irrigation, warfare, and trade. The premise was that linkages between population growth and technological innovation created social challenges that required the development of new social technologies—most importantly the formation (progressively) of villages, regional chiefdoms, and eventually states.

As a graduate student of Leslie White at the University of Michigan, Lewis Binford then identified social evolution as the major objective for which archaeology's material evidence was ideally suited. Binford and his followers focused on environmental, demographic, and subsistence changes among hunter-gatherers and horticulturalists, using functionalism. He called for a New Archaeology, an evolutionary and science-based approach to society emphasizing processes of adaptation.

Intellectually linked to British functionalism and Steward's conception of culture core, Binford's approach looked at cultures as adaptive systems working to maintain populations. A wide range of cultural traits—including ceremonies and burial rituals—and leaders (central decision makers) were analyzed for their adaptive functions as a cultural core.

The New Archaeology

The New Archaeology was a paradigm shift requiring a rigorous science-based field methodology. Methods to study adaptive processes incorporated multiscalar research design including statistical sampling in settlement survey, site excavation, and household archaeology. Systematic recovery and analysis of subsistence remains (botanical and faunal evidence, or ecofacts) were instituted, along with a concern for changing environmental conditions and available technology. Data collection became systematic using sampling, screening, flotation, and a wide range of new analytical techniques to study manufacture and use of tools.

Using the evolutionary typologies from Service and Fried, archaeologists often sought to classify archaeological cultures according to schemes of complexity and adaptation. Regional organizations with central places, monument construction, and wealth concentrated in a few burials were used to identify the central leadership of chiefdoms operating to solve regional ecological problems, such as redistribution of resources within specialized economies and the construction of mid-sized irrigation systems and monument architecture.

In England Colin Renfrew advocated new archaeological approaches to prehistory. He classified the Wessex Neolithic Bronze Age society with its famous central places of Stonehenge and Avebury as chiefdoms with a new regional social technology.

Influenced by their cultural colleagues at the University of Michigan (Sahlins, Service, and Wolf), Kent Flannery, Jeffrey Parsons, and Henry Wright sought to understand how and why chiefdoms and states emerged in prehistory. As an exemplar, Flannery's Valley of Oaxaca Project set a new standard for multiscalar archaeological research by looking at materialist and cultural variables—including population size (measured by the number and size of settlements), the subsistence economy (described by food remains, food procurement, and processing technology such as arrowheads, spears, knives, choppers, pestles, grinding equipment, and cooking vessels), and social organization (settlement hierarchy and specialization). Already interest was shifting to consider aspects of political organization, trade, and religion—as illustrated by Flannery's edited book *The Early Mesoamerican Village*.

Such studies documented the economies based on subsistence, trade and markets, and corresponding sociopolitical organization. Two problems continued, however. A reliance on social typologies became a goal to classify archaeological societies and to explain how a new form, such as a chiefdom, emerged from an earlier form. This ladder of social formations appeared to justify pseudo-historical typologies developed by cultural anthropology. Additionally, functionalism and its failure to consider agency as a means of selection proved theoretically limiting. Recognizing that societies subsumed different and often competing interests became central to the next generation of American archaeologists. What was needed was a better conception of agency as the mechanism for selection in social evolution.

PROCESSUAL ARCHAEOLOGY AND POLITICAL ECONOMY

Starting in the late 1970s, a second generation of New Archaeologists—many of them students of founding members—developed increasingly complicated understandings of prehistoric societies by considering issues of economics, social organization, political action, and religious practice. A rather large cadre created what became known as processual archaeology, for which social evolution was the central theme. Subsistence continued to be foundational: humans may not live by bread alone, but without bread they don't live at all. What was needed additionally, however, was to understand diverse and often conflicting agencies and group collaboration in multiple spheres of action.

Processual archaeology moved away from a search for prime movers—such as irrigation—and toward an understanding of intricacies in information processing, power relationships (Marxism), and economic theory. A promising approach was modeling multiple variables to try to figure out how and why evolutionary transformations occurred, sometimes looking comparatively within and between major areal traditions.

Parallel in many ways to Service's typology, Morton Fried suggested an alternative classification: *egalitarian–ranked–stratified–states*. In his egalitarian and ranked societies, cultural traits were selected by individuals and groups to solve utilitarian problems of survival and well-being. The selection process, however, shifted in stratified societies and states, adding top-down selection of traits based on their ability to assist elites to solidify power.

Fried explained how emergent political societies involved power relationships. Typologically, his ranked and stratified societies were similar to Service's chiefdoms but represented a shift in leadership roles from group serving to self-serving. Most important perhaps was his recognition that societies were divided internally into classes and factions, and integrated regionally and internationally into large networks of action. This understanding was inherently Marxist in orientation and reached back to the early work of V. Gordon Childe. Fried and Steward influenced a new cadre of cultural anthropologists at Columbia. Moving to the University of Michigan, Eric Wolf's work on peasants and traditional people affected by imperial expansion influenced a cadre of Michigan graduate students.

The Michigan School of Political Archaeology

Although they were students of the first generation of New Archaeologists, processualists were skeptical of integrated, goal-seeking systems. For example, when investigating the development of Hawaiian chiefdoms (see Chapter 6), I set out to test the leading adaptationalist theories of social evolution—especially whether prime movers of irrigation systems, regional redistribution, and warfare required central management by Hawaiian chiefs. My research showed that these propositions missed the central point that emerging chiefly power was based on surplus mobilization. Redistribution, rather than the central managed economy of locally specialized communities suggested by Polanyi and Service, was a system of taxation and political finance.

Research themes of processual archaeologists derived from economic anthropology and locational geography and several members of the group became active participants in the Society for Economic Anthropology. The material basis of archaeological evidence, of course, made it ideally suited for long-term comparative studies linked to social change. We took the lead investigating variability in traditional economies, understanding how interests of social segments and individuals were structured by social formations.

This generation of archaeologists included Richard Blanton, Elizabeth Brumfiel, Robert Drennan, Timothy Earle, Gary Feinman, Antonio Gilman, Gregory Johnson, and their students and others who became major archaeologists in anthropology departments across the U.S. We intently read each other's papers, participated in joint symposia, and developed ideas along parallel but often individual lines. As a group, we moved increasingly away from typological schemes, analyzing specific archaeological sequence with an eclectic mix of materialist theories from anthropology, ecology, geography, information science, and political science. Key was the concept of process—the relationships among economic, political, social, and religious variables that caused constant change based on selection of behaviors benefiting particular interest groups. We were dedicated to substantial fieldwork and analysis of archaeological sequences, thus studying real sequences of change to formulate and test evolutionary theories.

As exemplified by Gary Feinman and Jill Neitzel's comparative study of chiefdoms, these intermediate-scale societies were highly variable and it was this variability that we sought to understand. Processualists came to realize the functionalists' error that societies operated as self-regulating totalities. Rather, we recognized that societies were divided into competing and cooperative social segments (families, clans and lineages, special interest sodalities and communities of craft practice, elites and commoners, and more). This understanding of societies as divided both vertically and horizontally by conflicting interests and values became essential to realize how chiefs came to power.

As cultural anthropology moved away from materialist theories, however, processual archaeologists became marginalized within anthropology. In simple terms, just as we were beginning to sense that we had the theoretical, methodological, and evidential base to unpack the complexities of social evolution, a postmodernist critique against science-based materialism cut us off at the knees.

POSTMODERNIST CRITIQUE AND PROCESSUALISM PLUS

Although a minor part of research on social evolution during the 1970s, the pseudo-historical typologies from the 1960s became the justification to reject all evolutionary approaches as simplistic and Eurocentric. Social evolution became unpalatable to cultural anthropologists, committed as they were to cultural relativism and a recognition that societies contain such complicated interactions among age, gender, race, ethnic, and class identifications that any evolutionary scheme would be meaningless.

Part of a broad postmodernist critique of science-based research on human societies, many anthropologists criticized social evolution, cultural ecology, and economic anthropology—really all materialist explanations—as reductionistic and disrespecting cultural achievements of traditional peoples. Researchers instead focused on many social actors (elites and commoners, men and women, gender normal and gender personalized/highly individualized) who held distinct agenda and identities.

So different from the functionally integrated systems conceived early on by British structural functionalists and American cultural ecologists, these new relativists studied complicated and contested interests and identities that formed divisions of race, class, and ethnicity. Research shifted away from describing traditional peoples, because they were increasingly integrated into modern nation-states, and toward understanding contemporary societies as they experienced a postcolonial world.

Although most interest in social evolution in cultural anthropology was swept away, notable studies by D. K. Feil, Sidney Mintz, Peter Wilson, and Eric Wolf continued to work with materialist ideas, emphasizing a historical and evolutionary approach. Studies with the Human Relations Area Files compiled and synthesized anthropology's ethnographic corpus searched from correlations among variables that had obvious evolutionary significance.

Ian Hodder and the Cambridge School of Archaeology

As those dedicated to the historical science in cultural anthropology were censured as reductionistic, similar disparagement of processualism struck archaeology. In the 1980s Ian Hodder, his students at Cambridge University, and his followers sharply criticized a science-based archaeology. Calling themselves post-processualists, they made three salient points.

- Societies are open and complicated by issues of identity, sexuality, and the like.
- Belief in a scientific archaeology is wrong because societies are not self-regulating and contain many internal contradictions, personal agencies, and complicating interests.

- Evolutionary theories are wrong because they rely on a simplified, unilinear framework that suggests progress.

Processualists of that time agreed with many of these criticisms but maintained that the focus of post-processualist criticism was the New Archaeology of the 1960s, not the processualism of the late 1970s and 1980s. For a decade the post-processual critique disparaged social evolution and chiefdoms based largely on misrepresentations of the goals and procedures of our research. Post-processualists, however, were absolutely correct that social evolution was often misunderstood and misused.

Perhaps most telling was post-processualist criticisms of the evolutionary type (for example, chiefdom) as a distinctive social formation with common characteristics that could be ranked in terms of complexity. As documented by Feinman and Neitzel, although several archaeological measures can be associated with regional polities (chiefdoms), they are highly variable—such that the material record may be quite ambiguous.

This ambiguity is well illustrated in the cases examined in later chapters. Variability in chiefdoms reflects particular pathways that each has taken in the formation of regional-scale political order. Differences exist in particular mixes of three primary chiefly power sources (economy, warrior might, and ideology) and in the pushback that could be exerted by non-elites. Key is to consider how these powers are linked to the underlying population. I approach this within the framework of historical materialism.

Elizabeth Brumfiel at a Turning Point

In the title of her 1990 American Anthropological Association Distinguished Lecture in Archaeology, Elizabeth Brumfiel captured the desire to change archaeology: "Breaking and Entering the Ecosystem: Gender, Class, Faction Steal the Show." She identified social systems as composed of groups in fundamental conflict with each other, rather than as the integrated, self-maintaining systems portrayed by British functionalists and the New Archaeology. What was needed was evidently to move archaeology beyond the model of culture as a means of adaption.

This became what has been called processual archaeology plus. Stripped of the unilinear, typological, goal-oriented, and racist characteristics that have wrongly been associated with it, an evolutionary framework provides a theoretically strong framework to understand social change guided by multiple selective processes along multiple pathways—some involving the formation of variable regional political institutions that can be called chiefdoms.

THE BOTTOM LINE

A primary objective of anthropology is to study diversity in human societies. This requires a historical approach. One line of reasoning emphasizes relativism—that societies and cultures are historically unique with equally long histories developing effective and legitimate ways to handle everyday life, political relations, and meaning. From its inception, however, anthropology has sought cross-cultural insights that would help explain scientifically how societies change and diversify into different formations.

Social evolution as a theoretical approach came to prominence in the nineteenth century with the founding of anthropology. In the twentieth century, rich new ethnographies have provided the evidence to describe cultures and their variation. To explain cultural differences, a bottom-up functionalism is influential but is based on assumptions that cultures act as closed systems with goals. The Achilles' heel of the ethnographic approach is its reliance on social types (represented by societies that exist into the modern era). Without true histories of traditional peoples, understanding social evolution would always be problematic. To evaluate alternative hypotheses of social evolution, anthropological archaeology provides the diachronic database with which to test hypothetical explanations for societal change and diversification. The time has come for an evolutionary approach using archaeology as the main empirical base.

ADDITIONAL READINGS

Binford, Lewis R. 1964. A Consideration of Archaeological Research Design. *American Antiquity* 29:425–441. This seminal article lays out the framework for multistage archaeological investigations envisioned for the New Archaeology. Key was a shift in focus from excavations aimed at defining traits for archaeological cultures and toward studying cultural patterning as environmental adaptations.

Earle, Timothy, and Robert W. Preucel. 1987. Processual Archaeology and the Radical Critique. *Current Anthropology* 28:501–537. This article describes the post-processualist critique of processualism and suggests ways to incorporate its criticism in a redesigned archaeology eventually to be called processualism plus.

Flannery, Kent V. (editor). 1976. *The Early Mesoamerican Village*. New York: Academic Press. This book brings together chapters written by Flannery's graduate students at the University of Michigan in the early 1970s. It provides a useful summary of results from the Valley of Oaxaca Project, which became a model for large, multiscalar archaeological projects. The book expands the adaptational focus of the New Archaeology to investigate a wide range of social topics. It defines a transition to what is to be called processual archaeology.

Fried, Morton. 1967. *The Evolution of Political Society: An Essay in Political Economy*. New York: Random House. An alternative to Service's social typology, Fried develops a political economy perspective on social stratification and power. Like Service, it only considers the ethnographic corpus, but the approach became important to the next generation of American processual archaeologists.

Futuyma, Douglas. 2013. *Evolution*, 3rd Edition. Sunderland, MA: Sinauer. Futuyma summarizes concepts in evolutionary biology, looking carefully at the processes for evolutionary change that can be compared with sociocultural evolution.

Hodder, Ian. 1982. *Symbols in Action: Ethnoarchaeological Studies of Material Culture*. Cambridge, UK: Cambridge University Press. Ian Hodder is the guru of post-processualism, which he saw as an attempt to turn archaeology toward contemporary postmodern trends in cultural anthropology. This book is a well-worked ethnographic case for post-processualism, but attempts to develop a new methodology for archaeology proved to be problematic.

Marx, Karl. 1973 [1857]. *Grundrisse: Foundations of the Critique of Political Economy*. New York: Random House. This book presents the clearest definition of Marx's theoretical approach to historical materialism and political economy.

Mayr, Ernest. 2000. Darwin's Influence on Modern Thought. *Scientific American*, July, pp. 79–83. Mayr was a leading evolutionary biologist and his article lays out the importance of Darwin to changing western thought. Most important for our discussion is the identification of evolution as a historical science.

Morgan, Lewis Henry. 1985 [1877]. *Ancient Society*. Tucson: University of Arizona Press. Collecting descriptions of human societies from around the world, Morgan provides a typology of societies along a spectrum of subsistence-technological types. It is based only on contemporary evidence; anthropological archaeology had not yet developed to be able to provide actual historical evidence of evolutionary change.

Sahlins, Marshall. 1972. *Stone Age Economics*. Chicago: Aldine. Classic treatment of political economy from a substantivist perspective. Sahlins is a cultural anthropologist famous for his evolutionary study of Polynesian chiefdoms.

Here he introduces a multiscalar approach to subsistence economies describing the domestic mode of production.

Steward, Julian H. 1938. *Basin-Plateau Aboriginal Sociopolitical Groups.* Washington, DC: Bureau of American Ethnology. This is an exemplary cultural ecology study of family-level foragers from the Great Basin of the United States. It argues for highly creative, dynamic social and technological strategies to maintain a low-density population without agriculture. The concept of settlement pattern comes out of this work on societies as technologies of adaptation.

Ware, John. 2014. *A Pueblo Social History.* Santa Fe, NM: School for Advanced Research Press. Written by an archaeologist, this carefully reasoned book shows how archaeology can be directly connected with ethnography to see how societies developed in the American Southwest. Ware's consideration of social stratification and regional sodalities is significant to understand intermediate-level human societies.

Wolf, Eric R. 1982. *Europe and the People Without History.* Berkeley: University of California Press. A student of Steward, Wolf provides a dramatic comparative analysis of human societies as they became connected to the western world. He developed a non-doctrinaire Marxism that has been very influential to processual archaeologists. Wolf's approach suggests the historical contexts that must be considered to understand any traditional people. They are never frozen in the past but constantly changing in interactions with neighboring groups and foreign powers. His famous statement is that societies are not like billiard balls hitting against each other; they are open systems involved in constant change.

CHAPTER 3

CHIEFDOMS AND SOCIOCULTURAL EVOLUTION

Evolution offers a means to understand selection processes that diversify human societies. Although anthropology's ethnographic corpus continues to inform us about the many ways that human societies operate, only the historical database of archaeology offers diachronic and comparative data to study the diverging and parallel lines of long-term social change. Archaeology can contribute significantly to a social science of historical anthropology.

To undertake this worthy but daunting task, we need to establish the evidence for a substantial number of cases and evaluate them with equally strong and integrated theoretical frameworks. Because archaeological evidence is material and diachronic, it is well suited for comparative study of historical materialism. In this chapter I propose how diverse chiefly strategies combined top-down and bottom-up processes to build regional governing institutions.

ARCHAEOLOGICAL INVESTIGATIONS OF CHIEFDOMS

How can we study chiefdoms archaeologically? Often archaeologists have attempted to identify a list of traits associated with chiefdoms so that ethnographic analogies can serve to flesh out archaeological remains. Traits often used to distinguish chiefdoms include settlement hierarchies, elaborate chiefly residences, major communal labor projects, intensified food production able to generate surpluses, centralized storage of food supplies, specialized craft production of sumptuary goods, status hierarchy in burials with status objects, and the use of special foreign commodities.

Empirical work shows that these characteristics are associated with some but not all chiefdoms. A typological approach has proven to be inadequate because of the institutional diversity among intermediate-level societies. Chiefdoms should rather be studied and understood in terms of regional and centralizing processes of organization, control, and acceptance. The primary archaeologically measurable variables in many chiefdoms appear to include settlement pattern hierarchies, economic inequality, monument construction, and warfare. The significant variables, however, vary from case to case according to specific rather than opportunistic means for chiefs to build power.

Settlement Hierarchies

The first archaeological indicator of regional polities is settlement hierarchies with distinctive central places. Such hierarchies can be based on population size associated with different site types (hamlets, villages, and towns). Particularly important is to identify central places, a concept originally developed for market centers. At the lowest level of a market hierarchy would be the general store providing milk and bread, alcohol, gasoline, and perhaps a post office. At the highest level, special commodities like pianos or high-end furs and administrative services would be provided.

Central place hierarchies include a full range of functions: ritual ceremonies with special facilities, elite residences, hard-point defenses, larger population aggregates, and the like. Central places in chiefdoms, for example, included mound groups of the American Southeast, where ritual functions offered ceremonies for outlying settlements (see Chapter 4).

Centrality in settlement systems is often measured by the population living there. The log-log graph of settlement sizes often follows a linear decrease according to what has been called Zipf's law (Figure 3.1). The example is of

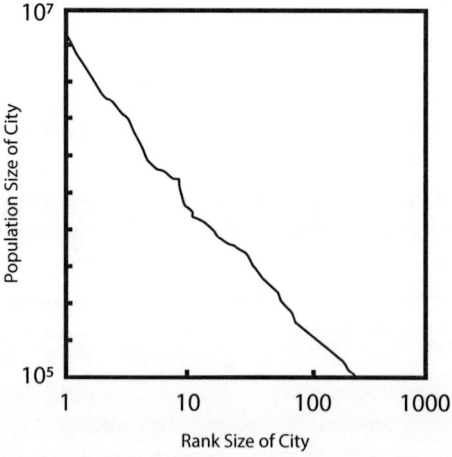

Figure 3.1. Using American cities in the twentieth century, this graph illustrates Zipf's law of decreasing settlement size (population) when ordered by the settlement rank from largest to smallest. This graphic technique describes the settlement hierarchy of any regionally organized society. The pattern is highly variable, suggesting variations in the political structure of society. Illustration prepared by Mark Hauser.

mid-century (1950s) American cities, when New York (first rank) was much larger than Chicago (second rank), which in turn was much larger than Los Angeles (third rank). In a log-log distribution of rank against size, Zipf's law predicts that each settlement should be twice the size of the next settlement in size. This curve can vary considerably from the linear pattern shown here to a convex pattern with several larger settlements of equal weight—suggesting multiple polities—to a concave pattern with a single primary center, suggesting strong political centrality. Robert Drennan designed an uncomplicated way to assess centrality: the percentage of a region's population occupying the largest (primate) settlement of a chiefdom. His analysis shows the extensive variability among chiefdoms in political structure seen in settlement hierarchies.

Not all chiefdoms are of a type, however. The largest settlements in the Wanka chiefdoms comprised almost ten thousand people, representing about 50% of the total population of the polity (see Chapter 5). By contrast, the central places of the Hawaiian chiefdoms were comparatively modest in size (probably only a few hundred) and represented less than 1% of the total population of a chiefdom (see Chapter 6).

Economic Inequality

The second archaeological indicator of regional chiefly polities is degrees of economic inequality implied by differences in burial practices and household consumption and/or size. Elite individuals often concentrated things of value and meaning that are routinely recovered archaeologically. When we first expose these exceptional objects, they take our breath away.

Concentration of wealth in a chiefdom or state can be measured by the Gini coefficient, which looks at the percentage of wealth by percentile held by social segments. This pattern is graphically displayed by the Lorenz curve, whereby the x-axis is the cumulative share of population percentiles ranked from poorest to richest and the y-axis is the cumulative share of total riches held by that percentile (Figure 3.2). The example in the figure shows how the bottom half of the group had only 10% of the total wealth. Theoretically, the line of equality (when every one has equal wealth) exists if the cumulative percentile of a population holds that exact proportion of the nation's riches. The extent of inequality is then represented by the Lorenze curve (observed distribution of wealth), which is the depression from that line. The curve expresses the extent of inequality as the amount of wealth concentrated in a few hands.

The Gini coefficient (a / a + b) measures the extent of inequality from 1 (top person holding all wealth) to 0 (total equality in wealth distribution). It can be calculated archaeologically by the cumulative ranked weight or count of symbolic objects (decorated ceramics, metals, exotic stones, and the like) in burials or hordes, household consumption of special goods (such as obsidian,

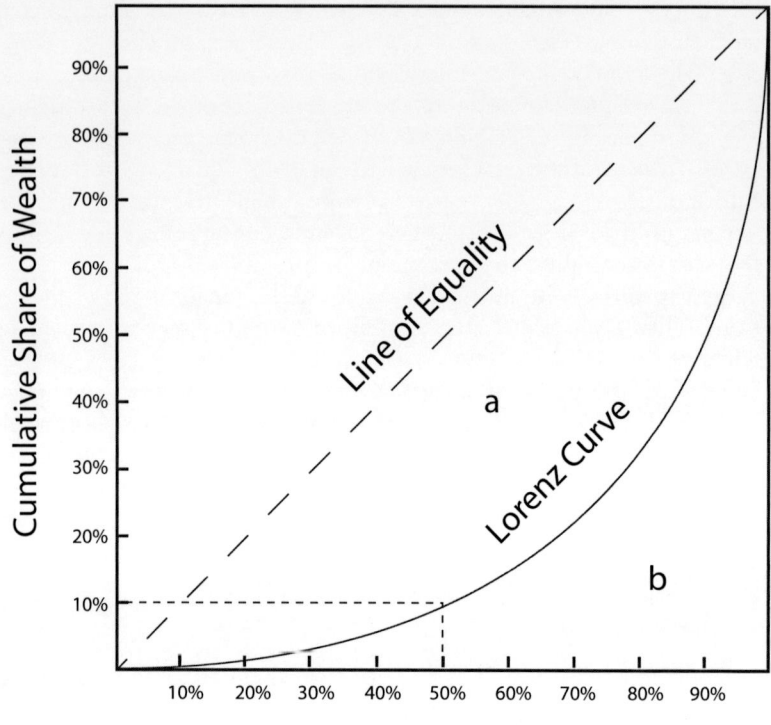

Cumulative Percentage of Group

Figure 3.2. The Lorenz curve illustrates the distribution of wealth in any society. The y-axis shows the cumulative share of wealth held by a cumulative percentage of the population (x-axis). The broken line of equality is the hypothetical situation where all people share the exact same amount of wealth; the depression of the wealth distribution (wealth concentrated in fewer hands) is the empirical Lorenz curve for a study. The Gini coefficient (a / a + b) measures the extent of inequality from 0 to 1. Illustration prepared by Mark Hauser.

fine pottery, glass, textiles, or metals), and/or for the labor invested in housing (from huts to palaces). The association of luxury items or finer housing with an elite segment helps identify the extent of economic inequality or social stratification.

Archaeologically among chiefdoms, the Gini coefficient differs significantly for different goods—for example, burial objects versus household consumption or housing investments. In Scandinavia, for instance, a hierarchy of chiefs is easily demonstrated by the deposition of incredible riches (gold, bronze swords, and other special goods) in chiefly burials, larger chiefly burial mounds, and impressive residential halls (see Chapter 7). However, not all chiefly hierarchies are represented by wealth objects in burials or household refuse. On the Hawaiian Islands, known historically as super-complex chiefdoms (or states), no unusually rich burials or large halls or palaces are known (see Chapter 6). Although a strong settlement hierarchy and monument defenses existed among the Wanka of highland Peru, the differences among elite burial riches, household size, and consumption were subtle (see Chapter 5).

Monument Construction

The third archaeological indicator of regional chiefly polities is monument construction. Like population size in a settlement hierarchy, it can be studied by scale of labor expenditures in construction of special facilities at central places. Construction volumes measure the mobilization of social labor—the people working to build public works projects including large ceremonial mounds, fortifications, road systems, and the like.

   Monument construction (even at quite small scales) requires institutionalized labor, obligations that indicate centralized authority and power. The amount of labor involved can be measured most easily by the area footprint of construction (square or cubic meters) or more accurately by the estimated labor—using ethnographic descriptions of the work involved and experimental archaeology—to complete the construction tasks. Analysis of the complexity of tasks such as specialized work responsibilities, overall design, and need for coordination are important. The total labor invested in a monument can be considered by construction phases; thus a large monument could be constructed with relatively modestly sized labor crews over several building episodes. This problem, however, is not insurmountable.

   The amount of labor invested in construction varies among chiefdoms, both in terms of the total labor involved and the particular facilities built. Mobilized labor can be invested in monuments, productive facilities (irrigation systems, terraces, fishponds), and/or defensive works. Often the amount of labor varies through time and between different cases. In the American Southeast, labor invested in religious, ceremonial monuments was high; on the Hawaiian Islands, although social labor built rather unassuming religious monuments, it is used principally to construct irrigation systems, fishponds, and agricultural terraces; and in Thy during the Scandinavian Bronze Age, an evident hierarchy (although modest) existed in labor constructing individual burial monuments and houses.

Warfare

The fourth archaeological indicator of regional chiefly polities is warfare, a naked power associated with most chiefdoms described ethnographically. Defensive warfare organized by chiefs can be identified by unusually high labor invested in fortification. The community as a whole benefits from these protective measures. Conquest warfare, by contrast, may exist without major defenses because large regions of internal peace are maintained by the chiefs. In such cases the presence of specialized warriors with exceptional weaponry is indicated.

As a third alternative form of chiefly warfare, raiding for wealth (linked to trading) is associated with warrior identity. The frequency and distribution of weapons (battleaxes, daggers, swords, and arrow points) help identify the importance of these cases. The extent of fortification among the Wanka (see Chapter 5), and of weapons and burials among the Scandinavian settlements (see Chapter 7), documents warfare with different objectives associated with chiefdoms with contrasting political economies.

To understand variability in chiefdoms and how to conceptualize the patterns of key indicators described above, we must grasp their political processes within a robust theoretical framework. In the terms of Adam T. Smith, chiefdoms operate as political machines to maximize—more or less successfully—power away from the people and toward a leadership structure. Margaret Levi calls this the predatory theory of rule.

The fundamental question is how and why do chiefs and subsequently kings come to power? This is a problem of top-down dominance, but it must be balanced in our analyses with a consideration of bottom-up processes by which people seek to avoid domination, assert authority in their own spheres, and co-opt top-down actions for their interests. The operation of chiefdoms represents a dialectic between these forces for centralized and decentralized power. There is no typical chiefdom, but rather a range of regional political forms that result from specific balancing dynamics of power.

TOP-DOWN APPROACHES: POWER TO THE CHIEFS

To understand chiefdoms requires an assessment of how chiefly powers are exerted over regional-scale polities. As I describe in *How Chiefs Come To Power: The Political Economy in Prehistory*, leaders can seek three elemental powers: the economy, warrior might, and religious ideology. Each source of power has its own institutional contexts and characteristics determining the political strategies that chiefs employ.

Controlling Economic Flows

Economic power provides the flows of resources and labor that are inherently controllable—at least in part—because of their material makeup, such that surpluses generated from the economy support power specialists and their institutions. But exacting tribute is not easy given the friction of distance and the option for families to escape control by "voting with their feet." The naked

force of warriors can seize and control productive resources and labor, asserting the right of the chiefs to surpluses; however, warriors can take things
into their own hands, kill the chief, and usurp sovereignty. Ideology is a system of beliefs that chiefs develop to legitimize their rule, but why should commoners believe the chiefly myths of divine rule? Key to chiefly power
strategies is always to weave together by material flows the sources of power
and thus create an effective political machine.

All power is inherently distributive, meaning simply that it tends to
spread out broadly across society's members. In traditional economies free-
holder farmers, fishermen, and traders act independently to manage their subsistence and entrepreneurial adventures. Each farmer, fisherman, or trader can
be his own warrior defending farm, boats, and other possessions. An individual can believe as he or she wants except when challenged by others.

For much of human history, individuals joined or exited social groups according to their perceived interests and associations. Communities had leaders but also—typically with the consent of their group—limits to specific
situations, such as the settlement of disputes to keep groups from fragmenting. In the largely egalitarian societies that existed prior to the emergence of
strong chiefs, individuals had fairly open (or at least corporately sanctioned)
access to all power to retain their daily independence. The revolutionary ideology of America stresses similar principles.

Chiefly power depended on controls that arose by intertwining the power
sources to create limited access to each. Control was not something inherent
in social conditions; rather, chiefs worked with technological and ecological
conditions to increase personal power. Most basic was control over the economy to mobilize surpluses to further chiefly ambitions. Key to understanding control of the economy is potential bottlenecks in the flow of goods
through the hands of chiefs.

A bottleneck is a constriction point in material flows by which chiefs mobilized surpluses for political uses. Sometimes such constrictions are geo-
graphic, such as limited fertile soil or major river routes or mountain passes,
but chiefs typically created bottlenecks by building facilities. In all cases a
chief must find a means to assert some form of property rights over the bottleneck. The medieval example is the castle placed above a river route, where
a "robber baron" sat proudly to collect fees for safe passage. The most common bottlenecks in prehistory were probably ownership rights in productive
lands and animals. For the Hawaiian case (see Chapter 6), intensification of
land by chiefly management of irrigation systems and fishponds created
chiefly rights to surpluses from those facilities. As described by Michael
Mann, landscape intensifications like irrigation tethered people to facilities
that were hard (costly) to leave.

Building ruling regional institutions by chiefs required a means to support
their institutions of power and integration. Terence D'Altroy and I outline
how governing institutions required top-down channeling of commodities as

a means of finance. We identified two means of resource channeling—staple finance and wealth finance. Staple finance involved mobilization of food goods used to support those working for the chiefs. Staple finance relied on corvée labor, in which commoners were obligated to work for their overlords, building facilities and producing goods that supported the elites. Wealth finance, by contrast, involved the amassing and distribution of special goods (prestige objects, weapons, and ritual objects) made by craft specialists attached to the chiefs or obtained from distances. For the Panamanian chiefdoms, wealth finance represented Jonathan Friedman and Michael Rowlands's prestige goods exchange (see Chapter 1). These special commodities were obtained outside the subsistence sphere and were not dependent on commoner labor.

Warfare and Religious Ideology

As depicted by Robert Carneiro, warfare was central to many—if not most—chiefdoms. Chieftaincies included highly trained and ruthless warriors who sought to enrich themselves in service to chiefs. As seen in the Hawaiian case, surpluses mobilized by chiefs supported conquest warfare of productive land and their dependent populations (see Chapter 6). Alternatively, warriors could be used to seize and dominate trade routes; accompany trading ventures to protect goods in transport; and raid for precious goods, including metal for weapons and slaves (see Chapter 7). Nikolay Kradin describes how the super-complex chiefdoms of central Asia used wealth obtained from raiding and conquest to galvanize imperial polities across massive areas. By controlling the distribution of wealth, chiefs were able to keep warriors loyal and bound to their chieftaincy.

Similarly, surpluses could serve to support priests, feasts, and elaborate ceremonies that expressed ideologically religious worth of chiefs. Provisioning ritual occasions legitimized rights and obligations to rule. As I argue in Chapter 4, the support of religious ceremonies by chiefs may have been one of the earliest means to establish legitimacy of centralized power and the right to mobilize surpluses. This is immediately relevant to cases of chiefdoms with dramatic, monument ritual architecture as implying centralized ceremonies and the obligations of a population to support its political and religious leaders. In some cases chiefdoms were essentially theocracies, but generally chiefs held divinely sanctioned rights of rule.

Power Strategies

As discussed in the ethnographic cases (see Chapter 1), understanding chiefly mobilization of surpluses in labor and commodities focuses us on power strategies, mixing points of control and compliance. Relations between chiefs and between chiefs and non-chiefs in their chieftaincies and confederacies are political, contingent, and negotiated. They involve finance to build and maintain loyalty and service. The degree of formal political institutional development in chiefdoms is limited and unstable, creating a near-constant cycling of the political structures that characterize segmentary societies. Although chiefs would love to consider themselves as centers of stable and persistent polities, the reality is structural instability. The weakness of chieftaincies as institutions, however, is part of their strength because they adjust rapidly to changing political and economic realities.

Although power in chiefdoms arises from particular economic modalities, the emphasis on one versus other sources of power gave particular flavor to regional institutional formations. This variation is articulated by Colin Renfrew in his contrasting of European Neolithic and Bronze Age political organizations as group-oriented versus individualizing chiefdoms. His two models of chiefdoms emphasize quite different means to mobilize resources and materialize social distinction. This variation is linked to the ways in which the political economy generates surpluses that are used to finance institutions with varying mixtures of power sources.

Archaeologically, the contrast between group-oriented (corporate) and individualizing (house) chiefdoms rested on distinct economic modalities that created different material signatures, which have confounded attempts to generate a simple trait list for a chiefdom type. Individualizing chiefdoms marked chiefly distinctions in wealth found in elite burials or houses; they were display (consumer) oriented. By contrast, corporate chiefdoms represented chiefly status by landscape construction that showed control over labor; these chiefs often did not display status by symbolic objects of distinction. When wealth was clearly stratified in burials, most would accept the presence of a chiefly hierarchy; but where wealth objects were little used, some denied that chiefs existed. This is a critical misunderstanding of the variability of chiefdoms documented by ethnographies.

Success of ruling chiefs depended on balancing powers and interests, dealing with circumstances that could change by the moment. Chieftaincies were highly adaptive, distinguished by specific economic formations and types of leadership; these "types" of intermediate-level societies, however, obscured their common regional and political nature. Hierarchy of chiefs was either of two levels (villages and the region) ruling a few thousand, or of three levels (villages, districts, and the macro-region) ruling tens of thousands. In either case the political bonds of the chieftaincies were highly personal, the local leaders at the village and region being closely bound through fealty to their ruling chief. Multiple hierarchies could exist in parallel within a society and power within the hierarchies was contingent and contested.

BOTTOM-UP APPROACHES: POWER TO THE PEOPLE

Although most archaeologists—who follow a political economy approach—have emphasized top-down attempts by leaders to control groups, bringing in bottom-up approaches is essential. Choices made by people in market-oriented, democratic societies have been theorized as a basic selection mechanism. This is the "invisible hand" of free markets that guides production and consumption decisions. Democratic "will of the people" shapes political institutions by enabling, restricting, co-opting, or evading centralized power. It is reasonable to expect that such agency would have existed to some measure in all societies.

Perspectives of non-elite agency have emerged from different theoretical strands of archaeological research. The popularity of household archaeology, for example, considers the extent to which families and their communities act independently of the ruling elite to solve most problems of everyday life. To account for the dynamics of social systems requires situating bottom-up political agency and top-down processes in a dialectical relationship, interdependent and potentially antagonistic. I draw on several bottom-up tactics that apply to chiefdoms: anarchism, house society, and collective action theory.

Anarchism

Anarchism and parallel approaches of heterarchy provide bottom-up approaches to economic and political organization, focusing on the capability (even propensity) of individual actors to self-organize and cooperate in diverse groups and coalitions. Anarchist theory helps explain the dynamics of segmentary societies often organizing as chiefdoms or even state-scale societies.

Aligned intellectually with Marxist ideas, anarchist theory addresses low-level local agency and processes and how regional polities emerge from local scales of action. Anarchism posits specific organizational principles that effectively counter centralized power: voluntary association, mutual aid, networking, communal decision making, and accepting useful authorities—but rejecting imposed power. Bill Angelbeck and Colin Grier conceptualize anarchist theory as explaining how individuals and groups self-organize to negotiate their interests with other groups and power brokers. Concern has typically been with communities protecting themselves from political domination by outsiders, but also from power-hungry individuals from within. Communities can resist chiefly rule or accept chiefs to fight against outsiders.

Heterarchical approaches similarly recognize competing interests of non-elite and elite segments, for which alternative sources of power effectively resist centralized political systems. Thus power may be distributed across multiple hierarchies from different clans, villages, or tribal regions, as well as age-grade associations, religious cults, sodalities, craft guilds, and factions.

With separate leadership structures, each social segment operates—to some degree—to realize its own interests in joint action. Chiefly authority is thus situational, consistent with anarchist ideas. Although a ruling sector might desire to be all powerful, chiefs can typically operate only in contexts (like the warrior chief's defense of community) that are considered good for the group.

House Society

Recent interest has come to focus on house society, a concept originally developed by Claude Levi-Strauss for the American Northwest, where bottom-up anarchistic theory has also been applied. House society has proven useful archaeologically because it represents basic socioeconomic units that organize much of social activity. Critical to the concept of house society is ownership of land and other resources (including rituals) by a house unit, which can be composed of both kin and non-kin members.

House-sized groupings exist in all societies, but to the extent that ownership or rights of access are held by these groups and not larger corporate associations, houses retain a high degree of economic and political independence. They act entrepreneurially to further their own interests. Archaeologically, as associated with inheritance patterns, burials should be closely associated with house structures—often under house floors, immediately adjacent to houses, or in the land associated with a farmstead (see Chapter 6). Analytically, house society links to the understanding of low-level agency described by collection action theory.

Collective Action Theory

Collective action theory is another, complementary approach in political economy that has grown out of Marxism to incorporate strong bottom-up processes. Foundational to collective action theory is Margaret Levi's predatory theory of rule, by which all rulers wish to maximize revenues to consolidate power, but in reality their ability to do so is conditional on counteracting the power of non-elite segments. Levi argues that elites, chiefs in our case, design their political strategies in accordance with non-elite roles in revenue (surplus) generation. Revenue from local populations—similar to staple finance—requires elites to provide services, such as building irrigation systems or temples, to guarantee compliance of farmers; however, when revenues are derived from foreign sources (wealth finance), no such reciprocity is required and elites act with less concern for those they govern.

Richard Blanton and his collaborators describe contrasting relationships between elites and commoners that represent what they call corporate (staple-financed) versus exclusionary (wealth-financed) strategies. In a remarkable comparative study of thirty pre-modern states documented by the Human

Relations Area Files, Blanton and Lane Fargher then show that the extent to which public goods were provided by elites correlated with local versus foreign revenue sources. An emerging theoretical consensus is that state formation is a process involving rational social action on the part of taxpayers as well as rulers.

> It is only with great difficulty that taxpayer-funded governments can be established and maintained . . . so that, in exchange for taxpayer compliance, rulers provide public goods, control the agency of officials (bureaucratization), and relinquish some aspects of their power (principal control) to validate their trustworthy participation in the collective enterprise. (2008, p. 252)

"Moral Economy"

While chiefs and kings might well want to act without concern for their populations, this is not feasible when the labor of common households provides revenue. Here thoughts of peasant rebellions come to mind. To obtain compliance (buy-in) from those who generate surpluses (commoners and peasants), leaders must provide local "services" (including constructing economic infrastructure, irrigation systems, emergency relief from disasters, and ceremonies that promise community fertility and divine production) since they also provide social pleasure and grandeur. When political institutions are funded by local agricultural production (staple finance), the basic labor power of the producers gives the farming sector power to resist overexploitation.

James Scott calls this the moral economy of the peasant. In his historical study of peasant rebellions in Southeast Asia, broad compliance required guarantees of subsistence security; the fear of peasant rebellions acted as a corrective to overly enthusiastic exploitation by landlords. Similar to anarchism, collective action theory describes how groups at all scales (neighborhood cooperatives to urban coalitions, oligarchic association, and political parties) shape political relations to resolve shared and competing interests. The key point is that ruling institutions depend on resources they control only indirectly, such that collective power of non-elite groups balances elite desire for predatory exploitation. Marxism's focus on dialectics provides the mechanism through which disparate components interact to produce social reproduction and change.

Summary

Balancing the interests and desires of chiefs and commoners, I recognize dialectical tensions between elite strategies for control and wealth accumulation (Marxist political economy); intermediate compliance, collaboration, and negotiation of reciprocal relationships (collective action theory); and self-organization, resistance, obstruction, and subversion (anarchist theory). The simultaneity of these social processes and agencies creates the tensions representing the selective pressures from different agents and their interest groups that shape the evolution of political formations under different ecological, economic, and historical contexts. For me this is the meaning of historical materialism and sociocultural evolution.

TRIBUTARY MODES OF PRODUCTION: FINANCING CHIEFLY INSTITUTIONS OF POWER

Chiefdoms are highly variable, but for comparative purposes I rely on their particular socioeconomic formations to help explain variability. In terms of evolutionary processes, selection by top-down and bottom-up approaches can be seen as alternative ways to understand economic modalities, with formations that create specificity in how economic and power relationships become intertwined. In the capitalist mode of production, for example, workers sell their labor to capitalists—whose ownership of factories, transport facilities, and institutions of finance allows them to channel flows of wealth used to realize political and economic power. My premise is that with variables suitable to non-capitalist societies, such an analysis can be applied to prehistory.

All chiefdoms are based on variants of what can be called tributary modes of production. Different modalities create distinguishing archaeological signatures. As illustrated in our case studies, modalities can emphasize alternative sources of power that gave particular flavors to different chiefdoms and a distinction in status marking between reliance on monument construction and wealth goods. I discuss alternative tributary formations to help understand the variability that is possible in chiefly political economies with alternative pathways to complexity. The selective mechanisms operating under different historical contexts route political economies along different paths of development.

Following Eric Wolf, a mode of production is the labor process that extracts, transforms, and distributes resources by means of the society's tools, skills, organization, and knowledge. The labor process is always socially organized, involving established relationships between working individuals and their groups (a social formation). Flows of commodities create social formations with degrees of stratification and unequal power relationships.

Sidney Mintz recalled Julian Steward's elegant expression: "When a specific technology is superimposed upon a particular environment, the social organization of the local group sets the limits of any possible variation of political forms" (2014, p. 499). While social formations are historically specific to a time and place, a mode of production is a relational and material concept that can be employed to compare historically different societies. Wolf's tributary mode of production, for example, is a generalized concept that applies to all chiefdoms and archaic states. By definition they rely on the extraction and deployment of surpluses to fuel political machines. Property rights (socially defined economic relationships to resources, technology, landscapes, and places) are key to understanding these different modalities.

The tributary mode includes different ways to mobilize and distribute surpluses. Any social formation typically has nested organizations of production. Thus a chiefdom contains a modality (a tributary mode) geared to surplus extraction, but it also embeds communities and families that operate according to their distinctive logics of house self-sufficiency and community reciprocity. Modes of production should never be thought of as a new typology; rather, they represent specific societal relationships grounded in material conditions that result in alternative political outcomes. They are processes—not types—that specify how individuals obtain resources to support, resist, or partially co-opt governing institutions.

This formulation provides the essence of a Marxist approach to anthropological archaeology. Modes of production represent abstractions of material relationships that model power strategy in political economies in ways that can be compared across prehistoric and historic cases. For discussions of chiefdoms, four tributary modalities are now considered. This list is not meant to be exhaustive or exclusive; instead it illustrates the continuous and changing nature of chiefly political economies and their social formations. Although discussed separately, these processes combined historically to fashion infinitely creative political strategies.

Ritual Mode of Production

The ritual mode of production (see Chapter 4) involves societies with variable population densities that can be supported by different subsistence economies including foragers, pastoralists, and farmers. Critical is the construction of ceremonial monuments, which represent ritual services provided by chiefs to their followers at the same time they establish ownership. Monuments are chiefly places because chiefs organize and support construction, renovations, and ritual performances. These are corporately organized societies in which chiefs can claim overarching rights to community resources sanctified by their responsibility to gain divine support.

Chiefs promote an ideology that these ceremonial places and their rituals, both dependent on chiefly management, are essential for renewal and productive fertility in society. Farming or pastoral families in such modalities retain a high degree of household independence, but they are thought to be dependent on their chiefs' ideology. The ritual mode of production represents what have been called theocratic chiefdoms and seems to have been the earliest modality to support chiefdoms. Mobilized staples support the labor process and related ceremonies and feasting of corporately owned ritual places. Archaeologically, the ritual mode of production is materialized by monument landscapes. To a variable extent, the circulation of special objects linked to ritual practice provided chiefs with additional leverage. These objects are characteristically associated with ritual hordes, not concentrated in burials.

Corporate Mode of Production

The corporate mode of production (see Chapter 5) involves moderately dense societies—typically horticultural—with intensive regional competition between communities for ownership of farmland or other productive resources like pasturage. Like the ritual mode of production, the corporate mode is based on group ownership of land but it emphasizes chiefly role in defense of property. This is the proposed bottleneck in political economy. Ritual is less vital in this modality but these corporate chiefdoms represent a spectrum in terms of sources of power.

Through staple mobilization chiefs organize and support construction of defensive work to protect land and people. Farmers retain personal labor power, however, and so chiefs are typically restricted to war-related actions. War chiefs are constrained and little marked materially. The corporate mode of production is materialized archaeologically by defensive works, which represent what I refer to as hillfort chiefdoms.

Asiatic Mode of Production

The Asiatic mode of production (see Chapter 6) involves dense human populations dependent on intensified agricultural production. Chiefs assert overarching ownership of productive facilities for which they manage construction and maintenance. Chiefly ownership of engineered landscapes is the primary bottleneck. Warriors are critical to maintain chiefly property rights and seize these rights through conquest. Commoner populations (primarily farmers) retain labor power as the only means to realize surpluses from agricultural facilities. In return for their labor, they retain guarantees to subsistence security in a "moral economy" and receive special services including efficient agricultural facilities and rituals that "guarantee" divine favor. The Asiatic mode of production typifies staple finance with mobilization from intensive agriculture, especially irrigated and drain-field systems. These chiefdoms represent a spectrum with the other modes.

Predatory Mode of Production

The predatory mode of production (see Chapter 7) involves lower-density societies linked to interregional and international flows of wealth goods. Most often they are part of a developing world economy, fringing agrarian states and to some degree controlling wealth flows destined for those states. Such economic modalities have various bottlenecks, including ownership of boats or animals used for raiding and transport; points of constricted flows in major transport routes; and knowledge in the productive process of special commodities, like metal. Farmers and fishermen have considerable personal freedom (agency). The labor process often involves slavery to intensify agricultural production supporting chiefs. Warriors are critical for raiding, protecting trading parties, and controlling constriction points. Ritual is also important to create significance of special objects that express status and meaning. The predatory mode of production typified wealth finance (prestige goods exchange) in exclusionary strategies of chiefly dominance.

THE BOTTOM LINE

To deny social evolution is a mistake, and—with increasing methodological sophistication—archaeology provides diachronic data for investigating this pivotal topic and understanding the diversification of human societies. To use rich archaeological evidence, however, requires theoretical tools as sophisticated as our field and analytical methods. To study the regional political institutions of chiefdoms, archaeologists should use political economy (historical materialist) approaches. Reasonably, most archaeologists following a political economy approach have emphasized the actions of leaders to control and dominate communities by coercion. This top-down approach is important but it is only part of the story of dialectical processes in chiefdoms.

Recognizing agency more broadly attends to self-organization that counters elite domination. Contingent political and social processes result in incredible variability in human societies and offer an understanding of creativity of human actions with the possibilities for social design, on which both Marxists and anarchists lay hopes. By stripping cultural typologies from social evolution, we can focus on processes of selection responsible for societal change. Gone are the social types neatly organized into evolutionary scales.

ADDITIONAL READINGS

Angelbeck, Bill, and Colin Grier. 2012. Anarchism and the Archaeology of Anarchic Societies: Resistance to Centralization in the Coast Salish Region of the Pacific Northwest Coast. *Current Anthropology* 53:547–587. Presents an anarchist approach to understanding the complexity illustrated by ethnographic and archaeological evidence from the American Northwest Coast. This approach is most effective to understand relatively small-scale political organizations.

Blanton, Richard E., and Lane F. Fargher. 2008. *Collective Action in the Formation of Pre-Modern States*. New York: Springer. Independently coding data from thirty historically documented pre-modern states, the authors show that the revenue sources (local labor versus distant trade) determined the extent of services provided by the state to its members. This is an excellent example of the use of the HRAF ethnographic corpus for statistical analysis of hypotheses appropriate for archaeological investigations that both authors have conducted.

Blanton, Richard E., Gary M. Feinman, Stephen A. Kowalewski, and Peter N. Peregrine. 1996. A Dual-Processual Theory for the Evolution of Mesoamerican Civilization. *Current Anthropology* 37:1–14. This article presents alternative political organizations (corporate versus exclusionary strategies) with contrasting means of finance (see D'Altroy and Earle 1985 below). These political strategies crosscut degrees of social complexity, meaning that societies at different scales have alternative means to organize themselves. Developing Steward's parallel evolutionary approach, this article shifts attention away from unilinear evolutionary typologies.

Carneiro, Robert L. 1990. Chiefdom-Level Warfare as Exemplified in Fiji and the Cauca Valley. In *The Anthropology of War*, edited by Jonathan Haas, pp. 190–211. New York: Cambridge University Press. Carneiro argues strongly for the central role of warfare in chiefdoms. Warfare represents both a means to create regional organization and to fragment their fragile institutional formations.

D'Altroy, Terence N., and Timothy Earle. 1985. Staple Finance, Wealth Finance, and Storage in the Inka Political Economy. *Current Anthropology* 26:187–206. Argues that political organizations require mobilization of resources for institutional support. A simple dichotomy is suggested between the channeling of staples versus values as strategies for finance; this dichotomy should be considered a spectrum across a range of empirical means for institutional finance.

Earle, Timothy. 1997. *How Chiefs Come To Power: The Political Power in Prehistory*. Stanford, CA: Stanford University Press. This book looks at three elemental sources of power—economic, military, and ideological. Chiefdoms are described as mixing the use of each, creating varying forms of chiefdoms. Contrasts are illustrated with archaeological examples from Hawai'i, the Andes, and Scandinavia.

Earle, Timothy. 2017. *An Essay on Political Economies in Prehistory*. Bonn: Habelt. (Distributed by Eliot Werner Publications, Clinton Corners, NY.)

This essay argues for a Marxist analysis in comparative studies of prehistory. Contrasts are made in the modes of production as representing contrasting political formations that are foundational to ideas developed in this primer.

Kohler, Timothy A., and Michael E. Smith (editors). 2018. *Ten Thousand Years of Inequality: The Archaeology of Wealth Differences*. Tucson: Arizona University Press. Wealth distributions are studied archaeologically with the Lorenz curve. Chapters cover different areas of the world, looking at wealth differences in both burials and household contexts.

Kolb, Michael J. 1994. Monumental Grandeur and the Rise of Religious Authority in Pre-Contact Hawaii. *Current Anthropology* 34:1–38. Article looking at the chronology of monument construction in Hawai'i associated with the development of complex island-wide chiefdoms. It is a good example of how monument architecture can be studied archaeologically.

Kradin, Nikolay N. 2014. *Nomads of Inner Asia in Transition*. Moscow: URSS. Kradin is a Russian archaeologist studying social evolution among pastoral societies in central Asia. Most importantly, he shows how the segmentary organization of pastoralism can be organized as super-complex chiefdoms by the distribution of wealth from raiding and conquest.

Levi, Margaret. 1988. *Of Rule and Revenue*. Berkeley: University of California Press. This book develops an important political science hypothesis that the source of revenues determines the nature of services offered by a governing body. Levi considers herself a Marxist, adding refined understanding of agency. Her work is foundational to collective action theory.

Mann, Michael. 1986. *The Sources of Social Power, Vol. 1: History of Power from the Beginning to A.D. 1760*. Cambridge, UK: Cambridge University Press. Mann is a historical sociologist focused on the long-term history of power and politics. He recognizes the different sources of power accessed by stateless societies. Although he considers his work a critique of social evolution, I believe it is part of that broader analysis but jettisoning simplistic, unilinear typologies.

Mintz, Sidney. 2014. And the Rest Is History: A Conversation with Sidney Mintz by Jonathan Thomas. *American Anthropologist* 116:497–510. Mintz is an influential Marxist anthropologist, best known for his book *Sweetness and Power: The Place of Sugar in American History*. This interview discusses his personal history with and influence by Julian Steward.

Renfrew, Colin. 1974. Beyond a Subsistence Economy: The Evolution of Social Organization in Prehistoric Europe. *Bulletin of the American School of*

Oriental Research 20:69–95. In this special issue on reconstructing complex societies, Renfrew articulates a distinction between group-oriented and individualizing chiefdoms marked by monumentality versus wealth distinctions in burials. I find these contrasting ways to materialize distinction critical to the dual-processual model developed by Blanton and to my modeling of economic modalities.

Robin, Cynthia. 2013. *Everyday Life Matters: Maya Farmers at Chan.* Gainesville: University Press of Florida. Using her archaeological research on Maya farmers at the archaeological site of Chan, Robin demonstrates the independence of their lives from the chiefs and kings living at the nearby classic Maya center of Xunantunich.

Scott, James C. 1976. *The Moral Economy of the Peasant: Rebellion and Subsistence in Southeast Asia.* New Haven, CT: Yale University Press. Analyzing historical data from Southeast Asia, Scott argues that peasants rebel not from oppression—which they take for granted—but when their subsistence is threatened. As long as their subsistence economy is guaranteed by the lords, peasants accept their exploitation.

Smith, Adam T. 2016. *The Political Machine: Assembling Sovereignty in the Bronze Age Caucasus.* Princeton, NJ: Princeton University Press. The political machine is the institutional framework for the political structure of chiefdoms and states. Smith uses this concept to describe the Bronze Age sequence in the Caucasus.

Smith, Michael E., Gary M. Feinman, Robert D. Drennan, Timothy Earle, and Ian Morris. 2012. Archaeology as a Social Science. *Proceedings of the National Academy of Sciences* 109:7617–7621. Based on the comparative study of long-term processes, this article argues strongly for archaeology as an essential social science. It provides a summary of a conference on comparative study in archaeology, which was aimed at reversing the trend to concentrate on specific area sequences.

CHAPTER 4

RITUAL MODE OF PRODUCTION BASED ON RELIGIOUS IDEOLOGY

The ritual mode of production existed in societies with variable population densities supported by many subsistence practices—from foraging to pastoralism and farming. Critical were sacred landscapes built to stage major ceremonies. Land ownership by corporate groups focused on such ritual places associated with group identities and origin myths. To the degree that these places were monuments, chiefs had a central role in their building, necessitating mobilization of labor. Based on ethnographic studies of monumentality, social labor was linked to feasting and required some overarching right by leaders to mobilize surpluses in a political economy.

Chiefs came to power by weaving together management of the economy, warriors, and ideology to solidify some measure of regional command. The ritual mode of production allowed chiefs to emphasize their role in religion. Monuments grounded people both physically and emotionally to places, establishing group (corporate) rights typically materialized by group cemeteries that implied inheritance. Monuments made property rights effectively permanent, much like legal deeds in states. The role of chiefs in building and renewing these places justified mobilizing surplus labor and staples. This was an important form of political economy that characterized many theocratic chiefdoms.

THE RITUAL ECONOMY

Material support of performance and associated shrines can be called a ritual economy—as described by Charles Stanish in *The Evolution of Human Cooperation: Ritual and Social Complexity in Stateless Societies.* Stanish offers extensive documentation of a worldwide sample of early complex societies that were associated with monument construction. Ceremonies evidently provided the means to form groups for social action, an argument that he grounds in collective action theory. Is this practical?

Low-Density Societies with Monuments

Often societies characterized by ritual modalities were quite small scale and low density, in which an anarchist argument would seem to be reasonable (but not always). At surprisingly low population densities—for example, in the early forager societies of Archaic and Woodland North America—social groups built major monuments. This observation can be embedded within a political economy approach by understanding how chiefs organized social labor for larger constructions.

Even at fairly low densities, warfare characterized some forager and low-density horticultural groups. An uneven distribution of productive resources—particularly good salmon rivers, rich nut groves, or pockets of better or improved soils—favored defense against outsiders. Neolithic societies in Europe, as a good example, are associated with finds of large arrowheads; because evidence of hunting large game was quite limited at this time, these weapons were likely used to kill adversaries. With intergroup competition, ceremonies evidently asserted land claims and a willingness to defend them. In traditional societies social events attracted allies, which were critical for success in war. Regional ceremonies may also have provided services, resolving subsistence risk and providing a good opportunity for drinking and dancing.

Organizing Regional Populations

By promoting an ideology based on central places, chiefs could mobilize social labor to construct monuments linked to ceremonies of social renewal and fertility. Of course the power of these chiefs was strictly limited to particular group activities, such as these ceremonies, but probably also would have included some responsibilities for group defense. For other activities involving subsistence and social relations, families and their kin groups would have retained independent action. My sense is that the relations of this economic modality should be viewed as a continuum with the corporate mode of production (see Chapter 5), in which the exigencies of chiefly defense appear to have outweighed those of ritual performance.

The balance between top-down and bottom-up processes in chiefly formations was particularly clear with the ritual mode of production. Such low-density societies might well have been linked to advantageous areas with rich resources—like good fishing grounds, more productive pasturage, or improved farmland—but any attempt to require families to produce surpluses for chiefs would have been problematic. Opportunities existed to resettle in unused or underused lands. This process appears to have created the expansive migrations described for foragers–pastoralists–farmers; families and their associations could move away from chiefs who were too demanding. The check on emergent chiefs is simply the ability of people, in relatively open en-

vironments, to distance themselves from political strictures—often referred
to as "voting with your feet."

Monument landscapes and associated rituals, however, created a positive
draw, binding people to place. To the degree that chiefs could assert an overarching right to land associated with these places, they could mobilize surpluses for political purposes. If this is true, early chiefdoms had ancient and
widespread distributions at low population densities that characterized many
archaeological sequences with built landscapes. For example, "megalithic"
landscapes with large stone monument constructions (like Stonehenge) have
been documented broadly in Neolithic Europe, in pastoral-based African societies, in early sequences across India and Southeast Asia, and throughout
the Americas.

Monumentality Expressing Power

Marxist archaeologist Bruce Trigger emphasizes the political aspects of intermediate-scale monumentality to express the power of a leader and the groups.
Although recognizing that construction must have been part of a general
social process, researchers taking a bottom-up perspective can obscure political elements of feasting and construction (as Ron Adams describes ethnographically in Southeast Asia). Monuments were built by the initiative leaders.
Monument landscapes of prehistoric traditional societies created ownership
rights, through which leaders could access and channel surpluses to magnify
attractiveness of and demand for ritual performance.

Using Brian Hayden's term for those with Type A personalities in fairly
small-scale societies, aggrandizers gathered prestige and political support by
feasting. Food collected from supporters for feasts showed a leader's organizational capability and attracts supporters. For those whose lives can be quite
tedious, hosting a fun party requires the collection and preparation of special
foods (representing elemental staple finance). This basic logic could have been
intensified to support larger feasts, labor crews, and the substantial work of
monument construction. Such events involving both social labor and enjoy-
ment were critical to forming chiefdoms based on a ritual modality.

Often associated with inheritance from the ancestors, monuments created memories that tethered people to the land and mobilized surpluses in
new political systems. For Early Neolithic societies—as exemplifying this
process—built ritual landscapes served politically not simply to express power,
but to create power by structuring labor relationships linked to ceremonial
places and their role in marking corporate rights and responsibilities in land
and associated resources. When construction involved major monuments, societies to some degree became centrally organized, and I feel comfortable calling these social formations group-oriented chiefdoms.

MONUMENT LANDSCAPES:
NEOLITHIC SCANDINAVIA (4000–3300 BCE)

In the archaeological sequences of northern and western Europe, early Neo-lithic people provide a good example of the ritual mode of production in the early development of chiefdoms. These first European farmers cleared forest patches for shifting cultivation and their animals—a process of capital invest-ment to improve land. Based on recent DNA work, these people were pre-dominantly migrants who took over inland areas without significant forager populations and then progressively pushed foragers to the margins. Settled life became linked to burial monuments and eventually rather substantial spaces including causewayed enclosures, earthen circuses, and stone and wooden shrines. As detailed by Lawrence Keeley, warfare characterized Early Neolithic European societies. The particular nexus of ceremonialism, warfare, and an emergent political economy seems well documented.

To illustrate the sequence of monument construction in Neolithic Eu-rope, I draw from a recent article by Magnus Artursson, James Brown, and me that describes ceremonial landscapes in southern Scandinavia during the Early Neolithic (4000–3300 BCE). Although population density was quite low, evidently below one per square kilometer, societies constructed ceremonial places venerating the dead.

"Neolithization" of southern Scandinavia was closely connected with the Funnel Beaker culture, which spread across large areas of northern and north-western Europe. Settlements of single farmsteads and hamlets were placed along rivers, inland ridges, and coasts. Residences were small to medium sized, fairly lightly constructed houses with associated pits. Broad similarities in Funnel Beaker material culture, burial traditions, and ritual activities suggest a trans-regional ideology with common religious beliefs that probably repre-sented broad networks of interaction. For our purposes this archaeological culture strongly alludes to a grounding in place with rules of inheritance of land and its facilities.

Ritual and Ceremonial Structures

Analogous to the ethnographic potlach of the Northwest Coast of North America and the Moka ceremonies of highland New Guinea, leaders may well have gathered people to negotiate intergroup relationships. Archaeology doc-uments Early Neolithic central gathering places eventually being built with considerable social labor. These impressive ritual complexes had pits filled with feasting debris, wooden palisades, linear arrangements of standing stones, and bank enclosures. They were associated with mortuary rituals themselves and surrounding burial monuments including long barrows, megalithic buri-als, and the like. The multiplicity of non-habitation features suggests diverse social and symbolic activities that allowed ritual visitation and interaction with descendants. Based on ethnographic examples, such formalized relationships between the living and the dead preserved inheritance of property rights.

Introduced around 4000 BCE into southern Scandinavia, cereal farming and animal husbandry allowed for gradually increasing population. Improvements in farming techniques, such as the introduction of a simple plow, increased yields with opportunities to mobilize foods for ceremonies. In optimal areas population densities doubled, creating intensified subsistence economies that may have provided aggrandizers with social and political conditions to amass surpluses.

Materializing changing rules of inheritance, a sequence in burial monuments is evident. Four Early Neolithic forms of burial markers illustrate increasing labor required for construction.

- Long barrows: earthen mounds over graves.
- Facade graves: long mounds with stone or timber fronts.
- Dolmens with massive upright boulders and covering stone creating a burial chamber.
- Passage graves with a central stone chamber and stone-lined entrance.

This sequence documents increasing sizes of stones requiring more people to haul and erect, and more sophisticated architectural designs requiring specialized skills in weight load and placement.

Already by 4000–3800 BCE, the first monument graves (long barrows and wood and stone facade graves) were erected in southern Scandinavia. From around 3600–3500 BCE, work crews then dragged glacial boulders—often weighing several tons—to build the first dolmens. Implying long continuity in use and meaning of particular burial places, these megalithic (large stone) tombs were sometimes constructed within existing long barrows. The long barrows and dolmens accommodated both single burials and burials with up to 4–5 individuals. From around 3500–3400 BCE onward, the megalithic passage graves provided repeated access for communal burials of up to 100–120 individuals.

The Early Neolithic sequence of burial monuments points to a particular landscape history. First and most obviously, they involved a new and changing engagement with the dead, suggesting that ancestral ties carried changing rules for status and resource access. Second, the shrines involved constructing permanent monuments that conveyed meaning across generations. Construction likely involved socially obligated labor geared toward establishing particular places with emotive significance that related living groups to their ancestors. Correspondingly, these reputed corporate property rights allowed the formation of sociopolitical institutions, supported by rights to surpluses—increasingly important for labor mobilization.

Objects of symbolic significance also became important in the Early Neolithic of southern Scandinavia and elsewhere in Europe. Regional and continental exchanges of large ground flint axes, exotic stone battleaxes, and copper flat axes suggest emergent prestige goods exchanges that elites could hope to channel. In certain areas of southern Scandinavia, specialized deep-shaft mining extracted high-quality flint for axes—sometimes made so large that they provided symbolic, not use, functions. Axes were deposited as offerings, often in caches in wetlands.

Such special objects became associated with ritual meaning, and as players in these distant exchanges leaders could be seen as agents of religious actions. Ceremonial occasions—likely sponsored by leaders— increasingly required mobilizing labor to construct shrines, support associated feasts, and procure symbolically charged objects often from a distance. Access to divine powers became increasingly directed through chiefly hands.

Increasing in number and scale, the monument landscape of southern Scandinavia took on a distinctive character. While the number, size, and density of settlements increased only modestly, by 3300 BCE the number of megalithic graves in southern Scandinavia alone increased to at least thirty thousand. Major gathering places further document increasing scale (and thus likely the number of people gathered together) and labor required (and thus the labor to be mobilized).

Our understanding of the Early Neolithic landscape of southern Scandinavia is rapidly growing, especially with rescue archaeology required during construction of train lines, roads, and the like. In combination with earlier studies of tombs, the new work yields a vivid picture of developing labor mobilization in Early Neolithic chiefdoms.

Almhov (4000–3700 BCE)

Located on Sweden's western coast, Almhov was a gathering site with pits, huts, long barrows, facade graves, and other ceremonial features. Although placed close to the seashore, subsistence remains show almost no use of marine resources—in sharp contrast to earlier foraging-fishing settlements nearby. Animal husbandry was important; faunal remains included cattle, sheep, goats, and pigs. Carbonized seeds of wheat and barley document cereal cultivation. Remains of wild boar, some deer, and burnt hazelnut show that hunting and foraging continued in what must have been a forested landscape. Around the site surprising little is known of contemporary residential settlements, but they appear to have been small, fairly impermanent, and sparsely distributed.

Judging from the earliest features at the site, the main activities were cooking, feasting, burials, and offerings. Many pits contained substantial quantities of ceramics, flint objects, and animal bones indicative of feasting. From these pits beaker-like vessels suggest beer drinking (commonly described in traditional societies). Close by the pits were seasonal huts.

The layout of Almhov emerged organically from 4000 to 3800 BCE. Pits and huts—probably temporary cooking and living areas for social groups—formed ten clusters that were arranged roughly around an open center, likely a ceremonial space. The first burial shrine was a large long barrow, circa ninety meters long and eight meters wide, with a post-built eastern front. Three or four more monument graves were then constructed, creating what became an impressive grouping of tombs. To the east of the graves were empty spaces (showing low phosphate values in soil samples), suggesting nonresidential and probable ritual use. No debris of everyday activities was found there. A stone platform (5.5 x 4 meters) was associated with deer bones and antlers, features commonly found in ritual contexts throughout Europe.

After an apparent 200-year abandonment, people returned to Almhov around 3500 BCE to bury their dead again; two dolmens were erected on top of the ritual platform, suggesting that these old features must have retained significance of place across generations. With (still-standing) long barrows and facade graves, the site became a notable place, having deep history associated with the dead and corporate property rights.

Döserygg (3900–3300 BCE)

Döserygg was located on a prominent ridge bordered by wetlands and streams. The site included impressive burial memorials and other ritual monuments. Little is known of contemporary settlements in the surrounding regions, but they appear to have been small and sparsely distributed. Animal husbandry and cereal farming were the subsistence economy of the people who used this impressive monument center.

Döserygg served as a gathering place for more than six hundred years across a three-phase sequence (Figure 4.1). In the first phase, from 3900 to 3600 BCE, the site was established as a place to venerate ancestors. The first ritual deposits were made in wetlands—a common practice in northern Europe—to the west of the site, where an irregular shrine was erected by raising upright stones that based on ethnographic parallels could have represented ancestors.

In the second phase, from 3600 to 3500 BCE, the scale and extent of construction and presumably mobilized labor increased significantly. Impressive wooden walls with at least nineteen burial dolmens were constructed along these palisades. The walls were not defensive but rather suggest borders for a processional way through the burial alignment, perhaps separating the living from the dead.

These walls had two parallel trenches 3–8 meters apart that have been traced for 640 meters, but evidently would have extended outside the exca-

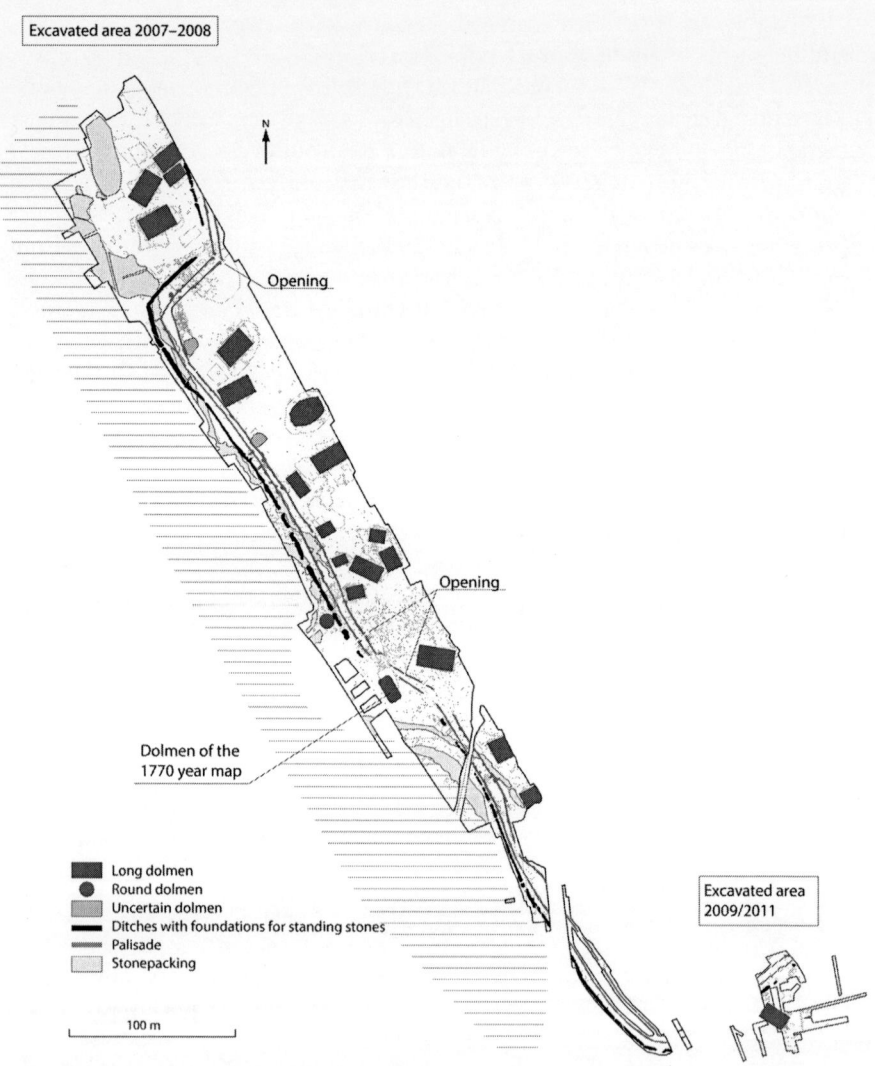

Figure 4.1. The megalithic complex at Döserygg (3900–3300 BCE) shows parallel wooden palisades probably defining a processional pathway, nineteen large burial monuments (dolmen) along the pathway, a long ditch for a row of standing stones, and extensive stone-packing along the west edging a wetland. Illustration provided by Magnus Artursson and Henrik Pihl, Arkeologerna, National Historical Museums, Stockholm.

vated areas. Well-preserved postholes for the post facades show 3–4 large up-right tree trunks placed per meter to create continuous wooden walls. The total number of posts required to build the palisades, just within the exca-vated area, can be estimated as 4,500—each requiring felling, finishing, drag-ging, and erecting. Three entrances, defined by standing stones and large posts, pierced the walls. Building tools (flakes from flint axe making, axe fragments, scrapers, burnt flint, and several broken whetstones for grinding and sharp-ening axes) were found in the trenches.

In the third phase, from 3500 to 3300 BCE, large burial long dolmens (15–22 meters in length and about eight meters wide) were built emphasizing long-term continuity, most probably of regionally based corporate inheri-tance. New construction along the palisades included hundreds of large upright stones, each requiring substantial labor and complicated task management to drag and place these heavy megaliths.

The long-term construction here of megalithic dolmens, double palisade walls, offering pits, and the string of standing stones created an impressive monument gathering place that was built and used for at least six hundred years. Construction must have taken place with a string of feasting events in-volving substantial numbers of people. Döserygg provided an imposing stage for regional ceremonies and displays of dispersed Neolithic people.

Sarup (3400–3200 BCE)

Causewayed (ditched) enclosures are large Early Neolithic sites that were first described on the British Isles and are known across Europe from Scandinavia to Spain. A combination of earthen walls, palisades, and ditches with entrance causeways defined these central sites. Enclosures were evidently ceremonial gathering places for sacrifice and burial. Some also served as fortified places documented by concentrated arrowhead finds around them. Sarup on the Danish island of Fyn was the first of these monument centers found in south-ern Scandinavia. It is still the best documented, built in two phases across a promontory. Many plowed-out long barrows, dolmens, and passage graves created a complex mortuary landscape near the site and contemporary settle-ments were scattered for many kilometers. The subsistence economy was based primarily on animal husbandry and cereal farming.

The first phase (Sarup I) dates to 3400–3200 BCE, later than the central places just considered for Sweden. Covering 8.5 hectares, the enclosure was surrounded by a wooden palisade with outside trench segments (Figure 4.2). The palisade was placed in a 1-meter deep trench that could be followed for 580 meters. In preserved waterlogged segments, the bottom wooden planks of split-oak trunks—sometimes nearly a half-meter across—were placed together to form a solid wall. The entrance was obscured from outside view by a fence, which would suggest either ritual seclusion, defense, or both.

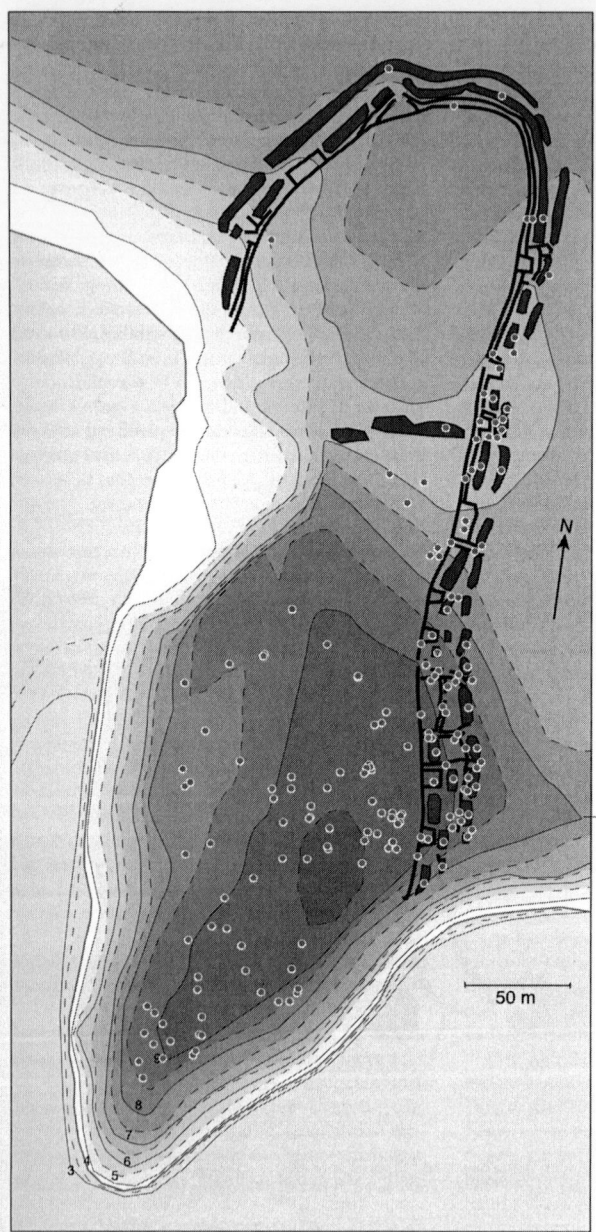

Figure 4.2. The causewayed enclosures at Sarup I, Fyn, Denmark (3400–3200 BCE). The enclosing wooden palisade is indicated by the solid black line and the two lines of exterior ditches by irregular black marks. Dots represent pit features dated to both. Illustration prepared by Mark Hauser.

Outside the palisade two rows of ditches and fences were broken up into detached parts, perhaps suggesting separate work teams from different social groups. Deposited in the ditches were ceramics, stone objects, animal and human bones, and burnt seeds. The human bones were secondary deposits, probably from surrounding megalithic tombs and brought together as part of a regional ancestral cult. Shortly after being dug, pits were refilled as formal depositions following feasts. Inside the enclosure were almost one hundred pits with remains suggesting feasting and/or offerings.

Around 3200 BCE the first enclosure was replaced by Sarup II, a smaller enclosure of three hectares on the promontory's southern tip. A palisade of smaller posts defined the enclosure with two rings of outside ditches. These were refilled incorporating ceramics, flint waste and tools, and animal and human bones (as described for Sarup I). Within the enclosure four postholes formed what could well have been a cult house. The bones of a young woman were found in two of these postholes; the bones had been burned at high temperature after the body had long been skeletonized, suggesting again that human remains from local graves were ritually treated. Clusters of megalithic burials surrounding the enclosure imply corporate kin groups.

SOCIAL LABOR IN EARLY NEOLITHIC MONUMENTS

Estimating labor in monument construction is essential for archaeological research on political economies. Size matters. It measures social labor, the primary currency in a staple financed economy. This can be called wealth in people and their obligated labor. The requisite labor helps establish the size of social groups from which it was recruited, most probably involving some leadership for task coordination. The Scandinavian sequence of monument construction documents the increasing complexity and scale of labor committed to the three central places just analyzed.

From ethnographic work we know that labor events were accompanied by festive occasions involving feasting, dancing, and socializing. A life of tedium in small subsistence groups was thus punctuated by social merriment. As discussed by Charles Stanish, ritual is a way to build social groups. The sequence of landscape constructions documented for Early Neolithic Scandinavia suggests labor mobilization as a means to form religiously based polities, which appear to have been rather unstable—repeatedly expanding and folding. Then, in these constructed places, subsequent ceremonials of renewal and ancestral veneration would have been socially valued and enjoyed. To the degree that leaders organized and supported all these events, they would have received prestige within their community and beyond.

Almhov

For the first phase at Almhov, when pits were dug and huts were built, no substantial mobilization of labor or resources would have been required beyond that offered cooperatively by kin groups (which probably held land corporately). When the first long barrow and ritual platform were erected, however, larger work parties were needed to transport material, build the monuments, and entertain participants. As more long barrows and facade graves were built, similar work parties, resources, and coordination were increasingly needed. Each construction event cumulatively built the landscape that bound living groups to the burial places of their ancestors. Engineered landscapes effectively mapped the countryside of polities that constructed them.

Döserygg

The physical attachment of groups to places made permanent by mortuary monuments created opportunities for control by chiefs. A qualitative increase in scale and task complexity suggests an ability to mobilize social labor with special skills and food for feasts. Although not all the shrines at Döserygg were built at the same time, the palisades and the first adjoining 6–7 dolmens were erected quickly without major interruptions—apparently constructed according to an overall design. An estimate of posts required to build the palisades, based on a section of 3–4 posts per meter, shows roughly 4,500 posts needed for the length of the trenches within the excavated area alone. If the enclosed area had been twice that size, at least 9,000–10,000 posts would have been needed. We estimate that the labor required for the palisades and first dolmens was perhaps 160,000 person hours.

Besides the manpower needed at the site, the labor must also have included many specialists—skilled miners to extract flint from deep pits, knappers to craft flint axes for the wood cutters, and those to organize task groups to move timber and stone and engineer heavy stone construction. Task management for procuring, preparing, moving, and raising the posts would have been significant. Most unskilled labor would probably have been obligated from local kin groups incorporated within a regional polity, but it is possible that prisoners of war could have been involved in such work (as described in Chapter 7).

Construction at Döserygg certainly required participation by a regional population and the mobilization of substantial food and other goods for compensatory feasts. To mobilize the more than three hundred workers needed for construction events would have required a total supporting population of between one and two thousand (one worker from each family of five). With a population density of 1–2 per square kilometer, this would require a support area of perhaps a thousand square kilometers, which means that ceremonial centers and their associated polities would have been spaced about forty kilometers apart—a common spacing for regional chiefdoms.

Across Scania in southern Sweden, six regions can be recognized based on the distribution of Early Neolithic stylistic differences in artifact inventories; these regions range from four hundred to one thousand square kilometers. Döserygg is located in the southwestern region with a size of one thousand square kilometers; this would give a population of 1,000–2,000 people, a figure that fits well with the estimated labor need to support construction of the site's most labor-intensive phase.

Sarup

Sarup presents further monument elaboration. The larger enclosure of Sarup I has been estimated to have required 100,000 person hours to build. The total labor demanded would have also far exceeded this estimate when all work on burial shrines and other demands are considered. The claim on labor was substantial. The causewayed enclosure itself does not seem to have been a long work-in-progress; rather, it was probably built and then rebuilt in one season (at least the major parts).

Such scales of work would have produced demands for mobilization of labor and materials that would seem unimaginable without regional leadership. For Sarup I, eight hours a day for sixty days, 208 workers would have been required, representing a population of around 1,040. Assuming a population density of one per square kilometer, this would have required 1,040 square kilometers of territory with a radius of thirteen kilometers—very similar to the Döserygg complex. And Sarup was not alone. As archaeological work progresses, additional central places are recorded.

Summary

The Early Neolithic of southern Scandinavia documents a history of monument construction from the beginning of Early Neolithic I through a period of population growth, and falling off quickly with a population decline in Early Neolithic II. During this 800-year cycle, local groups apparently engaged in intense interactions. By the time of Döserygg and Sarup, later in the fourth millennium, landscapes dedicated to ancestors and associated ceremonial cycles were well established. These central gathering and burial places show how the construction of landscapes became linked to relationships that probably transformed regional polities, despite their relatively low population densities. Regional organizations of perhaps a thousand or so people, a scale of simple chiefdoms, became standard. This model can be used to understand many small-scale monuments and their prehistoric societies from around the world.

MONUMENT LANDSCAPES: EASTERN NORTH AMERICA

Strikingly parallel to Scandinavia are monument landscapes of eastern North America. Ritual construction there had a long history, starting among low-density Archaic hunter-gatherers in the lower Mississippi River basin and continuing through Late Woodland Ohio Valley Hopewell, with a mixed forager-horticultural subsistence. Then the famous mound groups of the Mississippian culture were constructed with higher but quite patchy population distributions dependent on maize agriculture. Because no domesticated animals existed in eastern North America, hunting and especially fishing were always an importance source of protein in the diet. Extensive foraging and resulting settlement distributions were probably important reasons for distinctive economic modalities from the European Neolithic.

Archaeological evidence of chiefdoms in North America—similar to Neolithic Europe—relies on monuments, with little evidence for rich chiefly burials and social inequality. This pattern fits an understanding of group-oriented chiefdoms based on staple mobilization supporting ideological power. Through the North American sequence of construction, the support area from which populations had to be mobilized to construct mound groups was sizable and chiefdoms based on ritual modalities would seem to provide the best explanation for early monumentality. The materialization of their political and religious order in built landscapes, often with associated mortuary practice, exemplifies a distinctive pathway to complexity

Foraging Societies with Monument Landscapes

Mound building in North America began as part of the Archaic period of North American foragers, low-density populations utilizing extensive forested riverine environments rich in fish. The primary identifying characteristic of chiefdoms was the mound groups, which must have mobilized people from considerable distances. The non-local stone artifacts found at these mound groups suggest that participants came from a distance bringing a tool kit with them—as might be associated with pan-regional sites with secret societies. The earliest mound construction now dates to 3700 BCE along the Gulf Coast plain. Early earthworks were affairs located in bountiful environments with fish, nuts, and a range of other foods but with low population densities.

Logically, a forager economy here had potential for surplus mobilization, but a political economy with some centralized control would have been necessary to realize this potential to support large group activities, mound construction, and the religious-political systems they materialized. By 2500 BCE intense mound building began on the Mississippian alluvial plain at Poverty Point and another culturally related mound center in Louisiana. By 1200 BCE the massive Mound A at Poverty Point with a fill volume greater than 230,000 cubic meters was erected, apparently within a single year. Search for associated villages that could have provided adjacent labor, however, has produced only a scattered, impermanent site—showing that low-density foragers were capable of building sizable mound groups suggestive of chiefdom organization.

But how was this possible? Tristram Kidder estimates that Mound A of Poverty Point could have been built in ninety days with a labor force of 1,000–1,500 persons. Assuming one laborer for a family of five, a support population would have been over seven thousand persons. With a population density of 0.5 per square kilometer, the support region would have been about 15,000 square kilometers (70-kilometer radius). The implied political organization capable of such mobilization is perhaps unexpected among foragers, whose independent spirit is renowned. But it happened.

Hopewellian Societies

A thousand years later, during the Middle Woodland period (100–400 CE), the elaborate Hopewell earthworks were constructed in the riverine environment of southern Ohio. The subsistence economy at this time continued to focus on hunting, fishing, and gathering. Although horticulture existed to stabilize a hunter-gatherer economy, population densities remained low—as would be expected where starchy cereals like maize were absent. Without potential for intensification made possible with cereal agriculture, mobilizing staples for feasts and ceremonial occasions to accompany construction would have been challenging.

To sustain surplus food mobilization must have required an unlikely management of multiple harvests of fish, deer, domesticated plants, and nut crops. Because both the eastern United States and southern Scandinavia have relatively low—and perhaps risky—natural productivities, population densities at these early periods would seem to have been too low to support emergent regional political institutions. The records of demanding monument construction show this assessment to be in error.

Indicating regional (chiefdom-like) political organization, Hopewell central places were of substantial scale and architectural creativity. At least 170 Hopewell earthworks have been recorded in Ohio and Indiana, ranging from simple forms to complicated multiple configurations of squares and circles and often encompassing expansive areas. Unusually elaborate earthworks included the famous Fort Ancient, Hopewell, Newark, and Turner mound groups, each with striking monument landscapes. The largest single central place at Newark was spread over four square kilometers (Figure 4.3). A land-

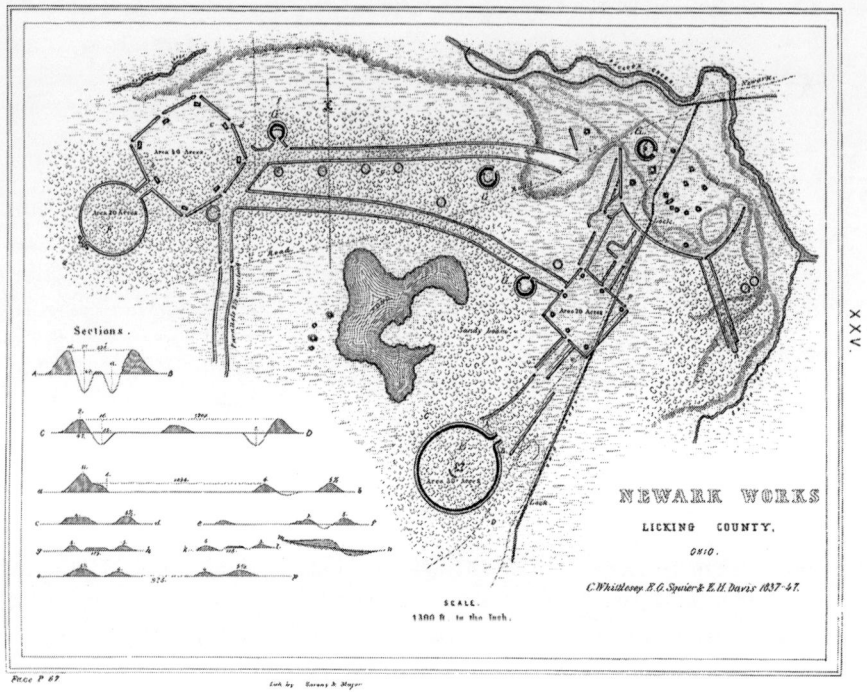

Figure 4.3. The Hopewellian Newark earthworks in southern Ohio represented in a nineteenth century illustration drawn by geologist Charles Whittlesey and archaeologists E. G. Squier and Edwin Davis, who surveyed the Mound Builder monuments of eastern North America.

scape architect was probably responsible for organizing the five ceremonial enclosures with connecting pathways. Particularly impressive were earth walls of one major component that enclosed circular and connected octagonal spaces of 2.1 and 20.2 hectares, respectively. Individual mounds were up to 5.2 meters high and enclosures were over three hundred meters long (approximately three football fields).

Complicated architectural designs evidently involved sophisticated planning using mathematical calculations for layout and sightings for astronomical orientation. The embankment walls of the octagon were ordered along moonrises and moonsets. It was actually quite common for monument places in chiefdoms to have had such astronomical alignments, which would place accompanying ceremonies within cosmic order (as made famous by Stonehenge). These landscape features—seen at Newark—suggest specialized architects and task managers; the impressiveness and sophistication of such ritual places, also found in southern Scandinavia, present something of a conundrum.

The relatively low-density, largely hunter-gatherer populations residing near Hopewell central places simply would have been unable to provide sufficient labor for construction projects, and regional organizations capable of mobilizing labor must have existed. The average population density around the earthworks was on the order of 0.4 square kilometers—consistent with dense hunter-gatherer populations rather than farmers—and almost all central places were without substantial residential occupations.

Large embankments such as the one found at Newark contained from 1,300 cubic meters to 25,500 cubic meters of construction fill and required substantial time (up to 280,000 person hours) to erect. For a single geometric earthwork shape—for example, a circle or square—to be constructed within a year, 1,000–3,000 laborers would have participated. In the words of Wesley Bernardini, "It would be difficult for construction to occur on neighboring earthworks in the same generation without drawing on the same pool of laborers, or drawing on very distant populations" (2004, p. 348). Assuming perhaps 200,000 person hours required for a single project, the labor force would have been perhaps four hundred people drawn from a regional population of two thousand. At a population density of 0.4 per square kilometer, a support area of about 5,200 square kilometers (41-kilometer radius) would have been required.

Although this estimate is surely conservative, the workforce needed for building the monuments must have required mechanisms to mobilize and reward many people coming from a distance. It is unthinkable that such work could have been based on coercion, because low-density populations would simply have faded into the forests.

The creation of a religious imperative could have drawn people from outside the immediate vicinity. The spiritual power and experience must have institutionalized a political economy through which leaders exercised rights to mobilize labor and amass food for feasting. Hopewell earthworks fit Colin Renfrew's model of locations of high devotional expression.

Hopewell's ritual modality also involved long-distance movement of exotic objects that were deposited as offerings or grave goods. These objects were special including obsidian from the Rockies, over 2,500 kilometers distant, used to knap a specific Hopewell biface. Native copper from Lake Superior was used to craft showy costume pieces, such as technically complicated ear spools. Sheet mica from the North Carolina Appalachians served for mica mirrors. Cups were made from marine univalves coming from the Gulf Coast.

Hopewell has long been recognized as central for extensive exchange or movement of sacred objects from foreign sources of power, as discussed by Mary Helms for the protohistoric case of Panama (see Chapter 1). High-status individuals may well have traveled long distances as part of their political networks, which gave them access to power objects that were incomprehensible to local people. In a subsistence-oriented world, these objects would certainly have carried a *wow* factor.

Mississippian Societies

Along the river systems of the Midwest from 800 to 1400 CE, similar political economies (monumentality and special exotic goods) supported the social order of the Mississippian people. Impressively large mound groups included the World Heritage Site of Cahokia, located just above the Mississippian flood plain east of St Louis. Across 1,900 hectares the site contains about 120 mounds, a defined central plaza space, and fortifications. It was the ceremonial center for a regional hierarchy of ritual places.

Unlike earlier mound-building cultures in North America, Mississippian societies were supported by intensive agricultural production of maize—a staple cereal crop. Warfare was cyclically significant, involving both fortification and significant casualties. The connection between higher population densities, warfare, and ceremonial construction represented an end trajectory for the mound builders of North America and a new emphasis on warfare (see Chapter 6).

What is evident for all these mound builder cases through prehistory is the religious foundation of their polities. These relatively low-density societies lived in forested environments with open frontiers where people could vote with their feet, moving away from coercive chiefs. Only the ceremonial draw, and probably some threat of warfare, kept populations loyal to chiefs. Even during Mississippian times populations remained concentrated in some areas, with other uninhabited areas not far away. These chiefdoms have been described as being both spotty and highly cyclical, developing in some regions and not others, rising to prominence only to fade away.

Using Mississippian polities as his example, Robin Beck describes constituent chiefdoms as opposed to coercive chiefdoms. His distinction means that Mississippian chiefs were embraced by a population because of perceived value-added roles—especially as intermediaries to the supernatural, from whom they could provide some guarantees of support against risk and uncertainty. By constructing monument landscapes, chiefs became leaders; the lure of the rituals, a break from the humdrum, and the implied messages of divine connection bound the group to its chiefs. In line with the bottom-up dynamics of collective action theory, the ritual modality chiefs who depended on their followers for revenue must have delivered services to legitimize mobilized labor and food.

THE BOTTOM LINE

The ritual mode of production characterizes many fairly low-density societies, providing a means to attract distant people to create a regional political system. Religious events and associated ceremonies appear to be the most common attractor, unifying people culturally and politically into chiefdom-scale polities. These theocratic chiefdoms construct impressive mound groups and other built landscapes that provide a permanent assortment of sacred places to which people are attached and for which they provide obligated labor.

These central places are stages for rituals to materialize the regional polity. Although all humans appear to hold religious beliefs, only under certain circumstances can these beliefs be transformed to support theocratic chiefdoms. Here I emphasize the foundational importance of the political economy. Although religion structures regional political identities, the built landscape materializes property relations that allow chiefs to mobilize labor and staples to support their theocratic machine—involving highly trained specialists in such things as astronomy and architectural design.

Charles Stanish shows the broad and early importance of ritual and monuments in human history. A religious-based ideology is remarkably common in more complex societies that included the Mississippian example at Moundville, Hawaiian chiefdom-states (see Chapter 6), and the early rise of complexity in Mesopotamia, Egypt, Peru, and Mesoamerica. Religious institutions supported by political economies are able to mobilize labor and staples in chiefdom-scale societies. As states form, however, the key becomes the separation of the ruling class based on god-like persona, stronger property rights, and accumulation of wealth as a means to signify distinction. This is a story of agrarian states emerging from chiefdoms.

ADDITIONAL READINGS

Adams, Ron L. 2004. An Ethnoarchaeological Study of Feasting in Sulawesi, Indonesia. *Journal of Anthropological Archaeology* 23:56–78. Adams describes ethnographically an Austronesian house society that built megalithic tombs. These monuments helped define the special status of successful houses with more land as able to mobilize and organize labor to haul and erect stones. These were stratified societies based on house ownership of productive land.

Andersen, N. H., 1997. *The Sarup Enclosures: The Funnel Beaker Culture of the Sarup Site Including Two Causewayed Camps Compared to the Contemporary Settlements in the Area and Other European Enclosures, Sarup,*

Vol. 1. Publication No. 33. Jutland Archaeological Society, Højbjerg, Denmark. This monograph presents the first full description of the Danish Early Neolithic central place of Sarup, which was used by Artursson, Earle, and Brown to develop their sequences of monument construction described in this chapter.

Artursson, Magnus, Timothy Earle, and James Brown. 2016. The Construction of Monumental Landscapes in Low-Density Societies: New Evidence from the Early Neolithic of Southern Scandinavia (4000–3300 BC) in Comparative Perspective. *Journal of Anthropological Archaeology* 41:1–18. This article presents the full argument on which this chapter is based.

Beck, Robin A. 2003. Consolidation and Hierarchy: Chiefdom Variability in the Mississippian Southeast. *American Antiquity* 68:641–661. Beck recognizes the distinction between coercive versus constituent chiefdoms. These are not subtypes of chiefdoms, but rather emphasize contrasting political strategies based on power dynamics in bottom-up and top-down processes.

Bernardini, Wesley. 2004. Hopewell Geometric Earthworks: A Case Study in the Referential and Experiential Meaning of Monuments. *Journal of Anthropological Archaeology* 23:331–356. With his knowledge of the American Southwest, Bernardini looks at the populations engaged in Hopewell geographical design monuments.

Hildebrand, Elisabeth A. 2013. Is Monumentality in the Eye of the Beholder? Lessons from Constructed Spaces in Africa. *Azania* 48:155–172. Hildebrand provides a useful description of megalithic monuments in Africa, demonstrating the cross-cultural significance of such monuments and the range of historically independent societies that constructed them.

Keeley, Lawrence H. 1996. *War Before Civilization: The Myth of the Peaceful Savage.* Oxford, UK: Oxford University Press. Keeley seeks to dispel the "myth of the peaceful savage," meaning that even among fairly simple tribal societies, warfare was an aspect of their lives. Warfare was widespread, offering opportunities for individuals to gain prestige and for groups to obtain and defend property.

Kidder, Tristram R. 2012. Poverty Point. In *The Oxford Handbook of North American Archaeology*, edited by Timothy R. Pauketat, pp. 460–470. New York: Oxford University Press. Kidder describes the scale of the early monument center Poverty Point that provided a ritual stage for regional political relationships. The scale of labor involved to mobilize and coordinate task groups would have required a regional organization.

Stanish, Charles. 2017. *The Evolution of Human Co-operation: Ritual and Social Complexity in Stateless Societies.* Cambridge, UK: Cambridge University Press. Stanish argues for the ritual foundation for emergent social complexity in chiefdoms and states. Ritual was materialized by early monument construction observed around the world, but perhaps most dramatically in coastal Peru.

Trigger, Bruce G. 1990. Monumental Architecture: A Thermodynamic Explanation of Symbolic Behaviour. *World Archaeology* 22:119–132. Trigger provides a historical materialist explanation for monument construction as conspicuous consumption to build and maintain prestige. This prestige would have involved both the group and its leaders in a political economy emphasizing labor mobilization.

CHAPTER 5

CORPORATE MODE OF PRODUCTION AND DEFENSE OF LAND

The corporate mode of production involved construction of fortified facilities that asserted a group's ownership of land. These "hillfort chiefdoms" defended the heights against neighboring groups seeking to expand their territories. Subsistence was usually agricultural and population densities were higher, requiring intensification with farming facilities like terracing. Labor and staples were mobilized from common households to support the construction of fortifications. This modality represents continuity from the ritual mode, but the centralizing powers shifted toward warfare.

WARFARE

Inter-village fighting existed broadly among agricultural communities—some quite small and others larger, but each defending land as its subsistence base. Bound by improvements in productivity, land was associated with corporate groups with inheritance rights signified by rituals of place involving ancestors. Fortified villages recognized that the local group would stand its ground. Warfare attempted to supplant neighboring groups and sometimes conquer them. The formation of corporate kin grounds and emergent war chiefs seemed to proceed together, often linked to ritual powers.

Leaders combined religious and warrior power in their political strategies but the mixes varied in archaeologically visual forms from case to case. Leaders could rise to power by emphasizing special status as builders of fortifications, regional negotiators, and leaders in battle. The role of leaders in organizing defenses and feasts for allies established rights and responsibilities to mobilize surplus labor and staples to build group prowess. This form of political economy characterized many chiefdoms in human history.

Warfare characterized chiefdoms in which leaders were responsible for defense. Population growth limited people's ability to vote with their feet. Robert Carneiro describes this as social circumscription, which he links to warfare. In such cases the balance between top-down and bottom-up processes involved guarantees of protection for the group in return for acknowledged rights to surpluses—such as first fruits or land farmed by community labor—due leaders.

My understanding of the corporate mode of production associated with warfare comes from ethnographic cases (such as the New Zealand Maori) identified by a warrior ethos, strong hillforts with centralized storage, and chiefs. The generalized model appears to apply broadly to prehistoric agriculture-based polities with strongly fortified central settlements. Examples abound in the archaeological record, but well-worked cases include the hillfort chiefdoms of Iron Age Europe and the Tell societies of Neolithic and Bronze Age central Europe. Such hillfort-based societies varied in size and settlement structure.

The elaborate fortifications that characterized some hillforts like Maiden Castle in southern England (Figure 5.1) created communities that were almost impregnable except against overwhelming force. Maiden Castle was large (nineteen hectares), the central place in a settlement hierarchy. It was defended by four earthen walls and ditches, with elaborate entrances designed for easy resistance against attacking forces. In the Castro Iron Age culture of northwestern Spain, for example, hillforts were quite small scale and equally sized. Warrior chiefs were probably important there in defending communities and organizing construction of fortifications and alliances, but their roles would have been constrained to warfare and community-building ceremonies.

These were societies organized against conquest, "societies against the state," fighting valiantly for community independence. In the Castro case, only the Roman imperial armies were able to overrun the hilltop redoubts. In some cases—for instance, hillfort chiefdoms of the Wanka—a regional settlement hierarchy was formed through regional conquest and subjugation. In this and similar cases, individual hillfort communities with sufficiently productive lands and substantial populations may have been able to muster fighting forces sufficient to defeat and incorporate their neighbors. But even in these cases the spatial extent of polities was limited. In highland Peru only the overwhelming force of the Inca Empire or the earlier Wari Empire were sufficient to defeat them.

Defensive Works

Archaeological indicators of hillfort chiefdoms included settlement hierarchies often with fortification, especially at central places (for instance, medieval castles). Corporate ownership of land often continued to be marked by group cemeteries but distinctive warrior or elite graves sometimes stand out. In regional polities weapons could become elaborated and used by specialized warriors. Many of these weapons were produced by craftsmen attached to leaders, and warriors could be bound to their chiefs by centrally channel-

Figure 5.1. Maiden Castle is an Iron Age hillfort (600 BCE) located in Dorset, southern England. Multiple ditches and earthen ramparts enclose nineteen hectares creating an impressive engineered defensive landscape. (1934 aerial photo by Major George Allen, public access)

ing gift flows in these weapons and distinctive gear. Warriors in chiefdoms were inevitably supported by the political economy.

Analogous to ritual monuments, building defensive facilities required centralized coordination to mobilize staple goods and labor. That groups held their land only in defense meant that warrior chiefs would have been considered essential and by extension held rights to mobilize surpluses from their communities and lands. Defensive facilities can thus be used to measure ability to organize labor and staple goods to support them.

Defensive facilities varied substantially in scale, ranging from simple earthen embankment and ditches to major stone defensive works that required much labor and task management. We can imagine the differences involved in the relatively simple tasks of building earth or brush enclosures, contrasted to the many steps with crews of specialists involved in shaping and hauling large timbers and stones for substantial walls. Elaborate defensive works often seem to have been out of proportion to their defensive functions. But in prehistory as for the archaeologist, the scale of defensive works served as a signal of a group's ability to organize itself and defend its land. The walls, like the monuments, declared power.

One frequent characteristic of hillforts—seen both among the Maori or the English examples—was centralized storage of cereals and tubers that could have served (among other things) for staple finance. Thus hillfort chiefdoms apparently depended on two key bottlenecks in the staple economy—ownership rights to productive land and the centralized flow of staples. Fortifications and associated war planning were offered by the war chiefs in service of their communities.

HILLFORT CHIEFDOMS OF HIGHLAND PERU

The Wanka of highland Peru is a well-worked historical and archaeological case for hillfort chiefdoms that I have studied with Terence D'Altroy and Christine Hastorf. During the Late Intermediate period, prior to the rise of the Inca Empire, the high Andes was fragmented into many small polities centered on hillforts. Most hillforts were fairly small with populations of no more than a few hundred, probably representing independent polities comparable to the Castro culture of Iron Age Spain. However, exceptional cases—illustrated by the Wanka of the Mantaro Valley—existed in which warrior chiefs conquered small regions to create settlement hierarchies in regional polities.

The Upper Mantaro is one of the largest and richest intermontane valleys in Peru's Central Andes. At 3,200–3,400 meters above sea level, the broad alluvial plain produced maize and (in modern times) wheat. Bordering the plain are hill slopes and rolling uplands on which quinoa, potatoes, and other Andean tubers were grown. Higher still, above 3,700 meters, is the grassland *puna*—pasturage for llama, alpaca, and now sheep. The ragged Andes and glaciers stand above at 4,400 meters or higher. Community lands cut vertically across these zones to support diversified economies, and this pattern of community self-sufficiency appears to have existed well into the past.

In a side basin of the Mantaro Valley, the Upper Mantaro Archaeological Research Project (UMARP) was organized in 1977 to study hillfort chiefdoms of the Yanamarca Valley. Its floor lies at 3,500 meters where frost poses a significant hazard to farming. In prehistory the valley's people built extensive ridged, drained, and irrigated fields to increase productivity and minimize risks—especially from frost and hail. In the period immediately preceding Inca conquest, intensive warfare characterized the highlands. The fortified Late Intermediate period settlements in the Andes attest to endemic fighting and war served as a primary power for would-be chiefs.

Working from an expansive settlement survey conducted by Jeffrey Parsons, UMARP studied the prehistoric Wanka people, who organized themselves into regional polities containing several fortified settlements—each with many households (residential patio groups). Our subsequent excavations sought to compare two time periods: Wanka II (1350–1450 CE) a period of regional warring polities, with Wanka III (1450–1533 CE) after Inca imperial armies conquered the valley. We excavated 74 elite and commoner households to reconstruct social organization and everyday life and studied changes in household economy resulting from imperial conquest and incorporation.

The Mantaro was an exceptional research area. It had vivid ethnohistorical documents describing the Wanka both before and under Inca conquest and unusually well-preserved archaeological sites that lay above the limits of modern agriculture, so that standing stone architecture was preserved. We were able to describe the region's political organization as hillfort chiefdoms and look at their incorporation through conquest into the Inca Empire.

WANKA II CHIEFDOMS: ETHNOHISTORY

Early Spanish administrative visits described Wanka society in some detail. Prior to Inca conquest, the Wanka fought fiercely with each other—led by hereditary war chiefs—and organized themselves into local communities embedded within regional polities. These historical accounts became the basis for my model of hillfort chiefdoms. Although of intermediate scale with a strong settlement hierarchy, the archaeological evidence is not readily consistent with a "typical" chiefdom. This case exemplifies the variation represented by regional polities and their political economies.

Two Spanish investigators described Wanka society prior to Inca conquest. They interviewed five elderly leaders and recorded general summaries of Wanka society. These informants lived under Inca rule and had knowledge—although undoubtedly idealized and romanticized—of pre-Inca culture from their parents' and grandparents' times.

Before Inca conquest, warfare was said to have been constant, waged among Wanka communities. They did not go outside the valley to fight but those of one bank of the Mantaro River fought against those of the other bank. Apparently, war's major motivation was to seize land to support expanding community populations. A community's wealth and survival depended on raiding, conquest, and vigilant defense against neighbors. When towns conquered each other, they would kill males and take possession of the defeated town and its land, animals, and women. In battle Wanka warriors sought to capture women for themselves, increase the community's agricultural land and herds, and build reputations for fierceness.

War chiefs were said to have led the Wanka community in war and, to a lesser extent, in peace. They had to be valiant and protect their communities from attack. Leadership passed from father to son but each new leader had to distinguish himself in battle. Power and wealth of a leader increased with success in battle. Although conquered land would have been held corporately by the polity and allocated to community households, victorious leaders divided the land and received substantially more. Valor in war and increased wealth in peace would have strengthened prestige and authority.

In a segmentary structure, the Wanka were organized into houses, communities, and unstable polities. Each house and community were said to be independent and self-governing, but communities were consolidated by alliances with and conquests of neighboring groups. Institutional power and scope of leadership remained problematic, however. Imagine opposing forces: opportunities for wealth and prestige through conquest versus intense cultural independence of households and communities.

Such an organizational structure described historically does not prepare us for the scale and impressiveness of central settlements observed archaeologically. Regional polities formed strong settlement hierarchies with large central settlements. Both the scale and hierarchy of regional polities were consistent with a broad definition of chiefdom, but the lack of material ostentation and ritual engagement were not.

WANKA II CHIEFDOMS: REGIONAL SETTLEMENT HIERARCHIES AND SOCIOECONOMIC INTEGRATION

The Tunanmarca polity had a sociopolitical organization, economy, and ceremonial practice with three scales of integration: the regional settlement system (the chiefdom), component settlement communities, and constituent households. I emphasize here the unexpected characteristics of internal disorder, ceremonial minimalism, and minimal institutional elaboration at the level of regional institutions. Warfare among the Wanka probably resulted in these apparently contradictory characteristics; despite processes of fragmentation, large and stable settlement hierarchies formed during the Wanka II period.

The Tunanmarca polity organized a sizable and dense population. Internal to the chiefdom were community specialization and intercommunity exchange, but communities and households independently organized substantial independence in everyday life. Settlement hierarchies were critical to determine the regional extent and organization of the Tunanmarca polity. Three research steps were involved.

- Identification of regional centers.
- Definition of lands and settlements associated with Tunanmarca.
- Determination of elite and commoner household economies at settlements.

Three major Wanka II regional centers existed in the Yanamarca Valley: Llamap Shillón (19 hectares), Hatunmarca (74 hectares), and Tunanmarca (26 hectares). The average distance between these centers was only six kilometers, less than a two-hour walk. Each center was positioned defensively on a high ridge, standing above and evidently defending prime agricultural land from the heights. Forming polyhedranes, territories associated with each center have been modeled by proposing lines marking equal distances between nearest neighboring centers and considering topographic features (streams and ridges).

Territorial boundaries of a polity were only a few kilometers from each center's defensive walls, suggesting the proximity of potential enemies eager to seize each other's land. The territories of each center contained land ranging in elevation from about 3,500 meters to above 4,200 meters. The location of these three centers appears to represent extreme population aggregations in competition for intensively farmed uplands, hill slopes, and bottomlands.

Considering Yanamarca polities, Terence D'Altroy proposes a three-tier settlement hierarchy.

(1) Central places like Tunanmarca had large residential areas with populations over 7,500 people. These were placed defensively, surrounded by multiple defensive walls. Each center had a small ceremonial core that included an open plaza—presumably for civic ceremonies—and some architecturally distinctive structures.

(2) Town-sized settlements like Umpamalca had smaller but still substantial populations of 2,000–7,500 people. These settlements were similar to the regional centers, with sizable populations and surrounding walls, but lacked a civic-ceremonial core. Originally, towns may have been centers of independent polities incorporated through conquest into larger polities.

(3) Fortified villages were substantially smaller, below two thousand people. Minor sites were probably used for special purposes.

Core territory associated with the Tunanmarca chiefdom was about 150 square kilometers, extending northerly into high *puna* where herding and perhaps mining sites existed. The Tunanmarca polity can be postulated to have contained at least seven major settlements: the central place, Tunanmarca; a town, Umpamalca; and five villages (including the well-preserved site of Chawín).

Demographic statistics for the Tunanmarca polity are impressive. Based on site mapping of preserved structures and excavations of household groups, population of the polity is estimated at about twenty thousand people, with a population density of 130 per square kilometer within the core territory. More than half (53%) of the polity's population lived in Tunanmarca, and more than three-fourths (79%) lived in that center and its secondary town with 5,200 people. The residual population lived in villages. This estimate of population size in the settlement hierarchy follows exactly what is predicted by Zipf's law of exponentially decreasing settlement size. The scale of the polity seeks comparison with the complex chiefdoms described for Polynesia (see Chapter 6).

The Subsistence Economy

The territory of the Tunanmarca polity encompassed a wide range of subsistence resource zones. The main subsistence crops were maize, quinoa, potatoes, and legumes. Animals consumed by Tunanmarca people included the llama and lesser amounts of dogs, guinea pigs, and wild deer. All plants and animals in their diet likely came from zones located within the polity's territory. The dominant source of calories was agricultural crops, grown on the land of the polity's core.

Tunanmarca's region contained intensified agricultural facilities—irrigation, drained fields, earthen-walled terraces, and ridged fields. None of these, with the possible exception of the irrigation complex, required task management for construction and use; they were technically simple and could be expanded as needed by houses and their communities. These systems, however, were embedded within an overarching political organization that defended property rights. Leaders were responsible for defense, a point made clearly by the ethnohistorical sources.

Landesque capital was quite extensive, certainly a major motivation for defense. Among capital improvements was an extensive irrigation system that linked at least six pockets of highly productive soils associated with settlements of the polity. Originating above 3,900 meters, the ditch soon divided into two main forks—one channeling water west toward a large village, the other moving water south past two villages and terminating at Tunanmarca. Ditches were simple: less than one meter wide, clay lined, and often supported by a stone retaining wall. Three rudimentary earthen and stone aqueducts crossed low points in the terrain.

The total length of the ditches was just over 24 kilometers and watered 100–200 hectares of high-elevation (more than 3,800 meters) agricultural land. Productivity on such land was threatened by short growing seasons that began with first rains, but irrigation allowed for predictable early planting that maximized length of the growing season. Ditches also provided permanent potable water to the hilltop settlements.

Other capital improvements found within the Tunanmarca territory included extensive areas of drained fields, terraces, and a small section of ridged fields. Yanamarca's valley floor was developed by drained fields with some areas still seen in aerial photographs. The most visible drained field complex is seven hectares within the territory of the neighboring Hatunmarca polity.

These fields formed an open checkerboard pattern of raised plots demarcated by surrounding ditches to drain excess water. Similar fields were evidently developed on valley lands in the Tunanmarca polity.

Simple terraces were constructed on pockets of gently sloping land. According to Hastorf and Earle, "The lynchet is an earth-banked field which was constructed by leveling soil and removing rocks to make a gentler slope for short fallow agriculture" (1985, p. 579). These were common throughout Tunanmarca's limestone-based soils. Additionally, directly below the village of Chawín is a small area of ridged fields, apparently used to lessen crop losses due to frost. Extensive areas of ridged-field agriculture have been described to the north of the Yanamarca, and such capital improvements may have been largely obliterated by modern potato farming.

Communities in the Tunanmarca polity were largely self-sufficient for food. All had access to agricultural lands and facilities that would have supported their populations, and Hastorf shows that each community's diet was somewhat different corresponding to immediately available resources.

The Craft Economy

Some communities of the polity, however, specialized in and locally traded craft goods (chert blades, ceramic vessels, and textiles).

Chert Blade Production

With availability close to some settlements but not others, specialization existed in chert blade production. Although chert blades were widely used for sickles, their source was limited to a quarry located on the western edge of the territory. Extending along a limestone ridge, the surface was littered with chert slabs, nodules, and manufacturing debris. In prehistory the slabs and nodules would have been picked up, initially worked to create blade cores, and then transported to a nearby settlement—where knappers would have struck off blades that were exchanged with other sites.

Glenn Russell describes community specialization in blade production by contrasting patterns from Umpamalca and the center of Tunanmarca. Both sites had similar densities of used blades, indicative of general service in agriculture, but they differed sharply in frequency of production debris that included blade cores and unused blades. Umpamalca had 23 blade cores from 283 excavated loci, while Tunanmarca had only one blade core from 456 loci. A production index of unused blades (either unsuited for exchange or stockpiled for eventual exchange) to used blades (showing silica gloss from plant cutting) emphasized the contrast. Umpamalca had a ratio of 2.26 unused blades to each used blade; it was a blade-producing site with close access to the chert quarry. The ratio in Tunanmarca was only 0.5, documenting a consuming site more removed from the source of the stone.

Pottery Production

Ceramics were by far the most abundant artifacts recovered by UMARP, with thousands from the many excavated loci needing to be washed, labeled, and stored on wooden shelves reaching the ceiling of our lab. As laboriously analyzed by Cathy Costin, ceramic sherds showed similar patterns to chert blades. She confirmed community specialization in Wanka-style pottery with contrasting indices of production debris to finished goods. The marker for ceramic production is the ratio of wasters (ceramic sherds showing extreme misfiring) to consumer-quality sherds times 100. Umpamalca's index was a relatively high 0.28 (many wasters), contrasted with Tunanmarca's index of 0.06 (very few wasters). Surface collections at the village of Chawín yielded no wasters. Within the Tunanmarca chiefdom, Umpamalca was apparently the main ceramic-producing community of painted Wanka ceramics.

However, Tunanmarca also appears to have specialized in a different ceramic ware but one that did not produce wasters in firing. The plain cooking wares manufacture at the center was documented by an extraordinarily dense ceramic dump in a single small test unit with over sixteen thousand sherds, mainly from these cooking vessels. Following this test excavation, what seemed to be a mountain of ceramic bags flattened the suspension springs of our pickup truck. We concluded that we had hit a dump of pottery broken in firing. Umpamalca and Tunanmarca were both ceramic producers, but of different functional forms that must have been exchanged between each other.

Detailed studies of ceramics sought to expand our understanding of production and distribution with the Yanamarca chiefdoms, through the neighboring Mantaro Valley and beyond. Petrographic analysis of nearly six thousand sherds showed regionally distinctive patterns. For local decorative ceramics, paste characteristics documented that materials used for ceramics from both Tunanmarca and Umpamalca were very similar, and together they contrasted with ceramics from the neighboring polity of Hatunmarca. Ceramics produced within the Tunanmarca polity stayed within the polity.

Some ceramic styles were traded around the Mantaro Valley. A special class of highly decorated ceramics derived from Wanka groups living 30–50 kilometers to the south in the main valley. But almost no ceramics came from outside the Mantaro region.

Textile Production

A few fragments of textiles were recovered in excavations; these were made of locally available alpaca wool. Documented by spindle whorls used to produce thread for weaving, villagers at higher elevations spun proportionately more yarn than those at lower elevations. Participation in textile manufacture was measured by the ratio of spindle whorls to 100 sherds (used to indicate normal household consumption).

At 3,800 meters Umpamalca had a textile production index of 3.0; at the higher settlements of Chawín (3,900 meters) the index was significantly greater (5.3), indicating more spinning; and Tunanmarca, (3,850 meters) had a low ratio of only 2.1, suggesting less spinning and perhaps receiving textiles as tribute. The inference is that higher-elevation sites, more closely associated with grasslands where alpaca were herded, partly specialized in cloth production from their wool.

Summary

Craft specializations were linked to resource availability and exchange among the settlements of the chiefdom. Umpamalca manufactured chert blades and decorated ceramics. Settlements located at higher elevations were more involved in textile production linked to herding wool-producing animals, and the central site of Tunanmarca made cooking wares. A functionalist theory for chiefdoms states that regional leaders redistributed products between specialized communities, allowing for increased efficiency in the overall economy. Redistribution, however, would require storage associated with chiefs, who would hold goods prior to giving them out—but no storage facilities for craft goods were found. Rather, intercommunity exchange was probably based on the simple reciprocity between neighbors that is associated with tribal societies.

On a regional basis, ceremonial activity in the Tunanmarca polity was not elaborately materialized. The association with ceremonial architecture (large open spaces, temple mounds, or distinguished burials of chieftains) has often been used archaeologically to identify chiefdoms. Using this pattern to uniformly distinguish chiefdoms is in error. As shown by the Tunanmarca, Wanka hillfort chiefdoms could have had little ceremonial architecture. Tunanmarca had special architecture that might have been ceremonial in nature, but it was not monumentalized.

Only the fortifications at the central settlement, its secondary town, and several villages were major constructions. These defensive walls, appropriate for a chiefdom involved in inter-polity warfare and defense of territory, defined settlements spatially and symbolically—such that walls could be viewed as community monuments asserting property rights by a willingness to stand their ground against others. The regional war chiefs served the local population primarily by maintaining peace, which allowed for "low transaction cost" (low risk) for frequent exchanges and protected property rights in improved land.

WANKA II: ORGANIZATION OF INDIVIDUAL SETTLEMENTS

A distinctive pattern of arrangement was evident in the settlements of the Tu-nanmarca polity. Here I describe settlements representing the different tiers in the settlement hierarchy: the regional center of Tunanmarca, the town of Umpamalca, and the village of Chawín. These single-component sites were built within a few generations and abandoned at Inca conquest. They were positioned on rocky ridges above agriculture, and as a result the architecture is remarkably well preserved, allowing detailed settlement mapping from aerial photographs and ground inspection.

As described by Elizabeth DeMarrais, Wanka II settlement planning—or its lack thereof—was consistent at all levels in the settlement hierarchy. Surrounding fortification walls defined sectors of concentrated residential housing. Irregular paths permitted movement across residential areas and gave access to informal neighborhood groups. Differences from one site to the next were in size, both of spatial extent and estimated population. Overall the appearance of each settlement was unstructured clusters of house groups.

Tunanmarca

Tunanmarca was the central settlement of the chiefdom that bears its name (Figure 5.2). The settlement was built high (3,850–3,900 meters) on a limestone ridge above the Yanamarca Valley to the east and rolling farmlands to the west. Within an area of 26 hectares, about 4,400 circular stone houses accommodated an estimated 10,000 people. Surrounding the settlement were one or two stone defensive walls.

Central to the settlement was a distinctive precinct with two open plazas (2,325 square meters in area), several houses, and an enclosing stone wall. To the east and west of the precinct ran narrow empty spaces that divided the site in half. These corridors, however, had no entrances on the plaza. Flanking the central precinct were two residential sectors with unelaborated entrances to the plaza area. To the north and south of the central precinct were large residential areas with enclosed patio spaces and interconnecting paths. The architecture of the site is exceptionally well preserved, showing the incredible density of stone houses (Figure 5.3).

What was this central precinct? One hypothesis is that it served for special chiefdom-wide rituals, an interpretation in line with many chiefdoms. Alternatively, the central zone may have been an elite residential compound—a large patio group for Tunanmarca's paramount leader. Because the size of the two plaza areas was too small for large social gatherings, only a fraction of the settlement's population and certainly that of its polity could have gathered there. Since the plazas lacked monument entrances and were not focal to the settlement's pathways, the plazas appeared as private space with restricted

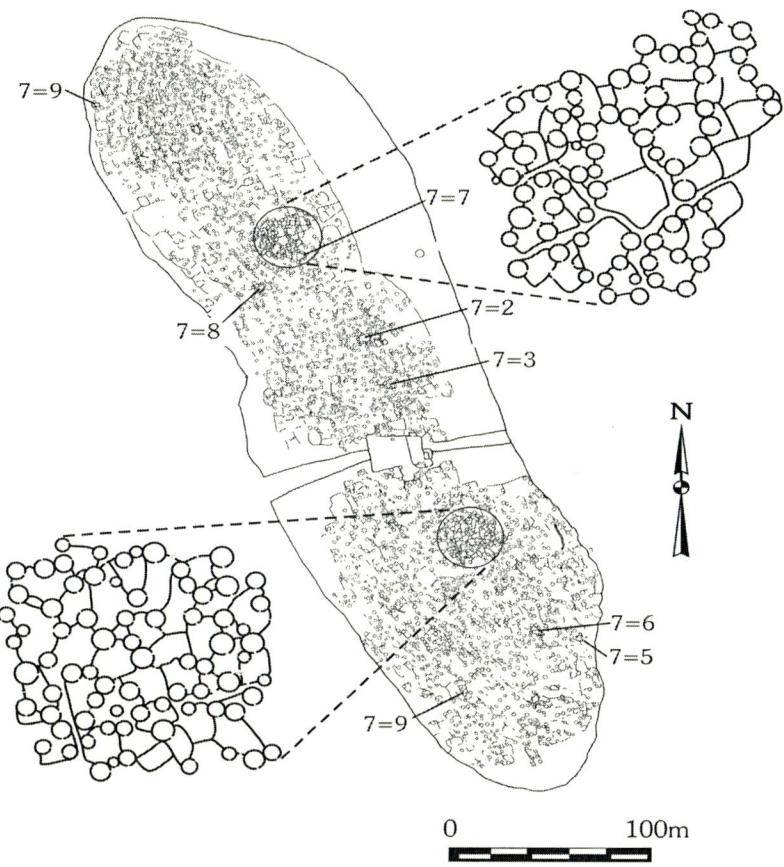

Figure 5.2. Map of Tunanmarca showing surrounding stone fortification walls, central plaza, division of settlements into two distinct settlement zones, and arrangement of house groups into informal neighborhoods. The excavated patios are all numbered. Illustration prepared by UMARP.

access. Ceremonies held there would probably have been personal, perhaps life crisis events associated with the chief.

Beyond the central plaza complex, the settlement's organization was almost unstructured. Two fortification walls on the west and one on the steeply sloping east encircled and defined the two settlement zones. These substantial outer walls probably stood approximately two meters tall and were constructed of limestone quarried from the ridge. Outside walls were pierced by defensive gates. Between the fortification walls was an open, unbuilt space, perhaps to corral llamas and alpacas.

Figure 5.3. Tunanmarca photo shows the stone architecture of houses that spread across the ridge-top settlement. Photo by Terence D'Altroy.

The settlement was divided down the middle by the central plaza complex and its open corridors. To either side were the two large residential sections of similar sizes (4,000–6,000 people each). The residential sections appeared as a disarray of circular buildings, but on closer inspection they were arrayed as small residential compounds that we call patio groups.

These residential groups were not organized formally; they did not focus, for example, on common plazas, burial monuments, or other facilities. Irregular paths ran across the residential areas. They were not gridded or arranged along axes; they did not orient toward plazas, entranceways, or other features. Paths simply provided direct access to some—but not all—patio groups. Many groups, however, were accessible only through other patios. As discussed for segmentary societies, each patio group implied an elemental house unit associated informally into neighborhoods.

Umpamalca

Umpamalca was the only town-sized settlement of the polity. It was built at 3,800 meters on a low limestone knoll with a sheer drop down to a stream; the site was positioned strategically near this natural boundary that separated two warring chiefdoms. From this position the settlement could have defended its agricultural land, animals, and women. In an area of fifteen hectares, about

2,150 circular stone structures housed an estimated 5,200 people. Umpamalca was equivalent in size and organization to one of Tunanmarca's sectors.

Umpamalca was defined by its fortification wall, which enclosed the settlement (except along the western edge with its sheer cliff). Several gates entered into the residential zone. Within the fortification wall was one large residential section with circular buildings of typical size and construction. Without a second wall, no enclosed open space would have corralled animals. Perhaps this relatively lower-elevation settlement had fewer animals.

Residential buildings clustered into small household groups defined by enclosing walls, a common patio space, and a few structures. No plazas or burial monuments existed at this site. The irregular networks of paths had no evident axial order or other pattern. They provided irregular access between patio groups and may also have divided the site into informal neighborhoods. Outside the wall was a small, undefended cluster of twenty or so residential structures.

Chawín

Chawín was one of five villages that formed an arch of smaller settlements west and north of Tunanmarca. The population of each village was around 800 (estimated range 600–1,450) persons and combined they approximated the size of Umpamalca. Chawín itself was built at 3,900 meters on a limestone hilltop to the north of Tunanmarca, overlooking the upper section of the Yanamarca Valley. The settlement stood strategically above the region's irrigation system and a well-constructed trail led down from the settlement toward Tunanmarca. Within an area of 5.6 hectares were about 420 circular buildings, housing an estimated 650 people.

Chawín was a small version of Umpamalca. Two fortification walls enclosed the settlement, except along the eastern edge where a sheer drop protected the settlement. At several points gates provided restricted access. The outer wall created enclosed spaces, perhaps for animals. Within the inner wall, the single residential area contained a typical hodgepodge of circular buildings grouped around patios. No common plazas or burial monuments existed. Crisscrossing the residential sector were paths that lacked a formal pattern, but they provided access to patio groups and may also have divided the site into neighborhoods.

WANKA II: SETTLEMENT PLANS

Following the analytical scheme of Bill Hillier and Julienne Hanson, DeMarrais provides a statistical description of Tunanmarca, Umpamalca, and Chawín's settlement plans. Two important points become clear: (a) the settlements did not approximate either a grid or axial arrangement and (b) the three sites—regardless of size and position in the settlement hierarchy—were organized remarkably similarly. Arrangements showed little centrality, even at Tunanmarca with its central plaza. Rather, they were agglomerations of varying size but with little internal structure. This settlement structure emphasized the paucity of ceremonial features like central plazas, mounds, or burial monuments that could have provided a visual or ritual structure for relationships.

Populations of different sizes clustered together rather chaotically; little evidence exists for top-down planning, except for the definition by defensive walls. The impression is of people coming together for defense but retaining a remarkable degree of independence in everyday life. This lack of pattern seems characteristic of chiefdoms with intergroup warfare.

As described for highland Burma (see Chapter 1), social organization appears to have been segmentary, organizing communities of varying sizes. These are what the ethnohistorical sources referred to as pueblos. Groups may have been arranged by principles of duality (upper and lower) that have been described ethnographically in the Andes. Separating Tunanmarca's residential areas into two discrete sectors seems to illustrate such an organization, and a similar dual structure existed at the nearby center of Hatunmarca. Tunanmarca contained roughly half of the chiefdom's total population. The other half was itself divided approximately equally into a southern population at Umpamalca and a northeastern agglomeration of villages.

WANKA III: THE HOUSE

The house was the family unit that comprised these residential communities. House structures and enclosed patio spaces appear to have materialized basic socioeconomic kin groups that conducted most activities of everyday life. The Wanka were organized by a domestic mode of production (see Chapter 3) in which households sought to maintain self-sufficiency by having rights to needed resources and maintaining labor for required tasks. These patio (house) groups were really quite uniform in basic structure.

DeMarrais provides a comprehensive architectural analysis of these units. The patio group includes residential stone structures on a common patio that was enclosed by standing walls, terrace walls, and houses (Figure 5.4). Excepting two rectangular structures in Tunanmarca's central complex, all structures were circular. A single doorway entered each house. Walls were double-faced, about half a meter wide, roughly coursed, and set in mud mortar. The average diameter of a structure was 3–4 meters with a roofed space of about 9–10 square meters. The number of structures varied from one to six but most had only one or two houses. Structures were undifferentiated in basic functions with hearths for heat and cooking and subfloor burials. With only one or two narrow entrances, these groupings created private spaces.

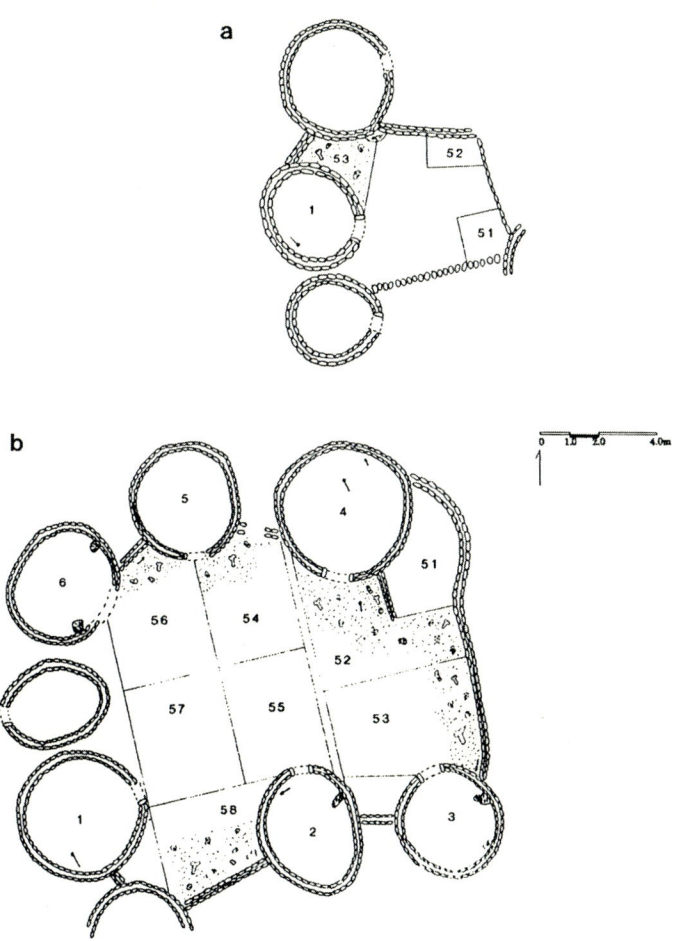

Figure 5.4. Illustration of two Tunanmarca patio groups. These house units composed most of a Wanka II settlement. The patio group with a single residential structure (a) is most common, likely for a commoner family; those with multiple residential structures (b) likely housed chiefly families. Illustration by Cathy Lynne Costin.

Differences between elite and commoner houses were subtle but still significant. Elite houses were located centrally within a settlement and their stone architecture was noticeably finer with careful coursing, chinking, and stone shaping. The main difference between patio groups was the number of houses. Each house was apparently a modular residential unit for one family. The patio group with multiple houses could then have been an extended family—several generations living together—or a polygynous family (each structure housing separate wives and children). If elites had special access to women, as discussed in historical documents, the larger housing units probably belonged to war chiefs. Criteria of location, size, and architectural quality guided the selection of patio groupings for excavations.

Status Distinction in Houses

Within each patio grouping was evidence for production and consumption. D'Altroy and Hastorf's book *Empire and Domestic Economy* analyzes variation in household consumption (animal bones and burnt plant remains, used stone tools, broken pots, and various dress) and production (lithic waste, grinding stones, spindle whorls, and less commonly ceramic wasters). Household trash from all patio groups contained basically the same food remains, used tools, and objects of display. Food, vessels, and even wealth were broadly similar.

Quantitatively, however, high-value symbolic items (silver and copper *tupu* pins and small disks) were more common in elite households. Elites ate more desirable foods such as deer meat, used more decorative pottery including both local and traded styles, and had more prestige objects of personal ornamentation. While households shared common patterns of consumption, elites were somewhat more ostentatious. All Wanka were equals but some were more equal than others.

Although households—both elite and commoner—were generalized economically, some specialized also in production for exchange. Part-time specialists were embedded within generalized Wanka householding activities, probably as a means to obtain things not immediately available. At Umpamalca six excavated households had a waster index that varied from 0 (one case) to 1.14. By contrast, within Tunanmarca the eight households varied from 0 (three cases) to 0.25. Even within a pattern of community-level specialization, specialized activities were small scale and restricted to a few households.

Specialized production of wealth objects was low volume and broadly distributed with little concentration in elite households. In our study of chiefdoms, production of wealth items—described for the ritual mode of production—is considered of great significance, because it offered leaders possible control of meaning and objects that materialized it. What we looked for was evidence of association between elite households and wealth production, but wealth production here was not associated with attached craftsmen.

Prestige goods were relatively rare and often were imported. Local decorated Wanka ceramics were certainly concentrated in elite households, but production was apparently not controlled by elite households, which had low waster indices ranging from 0.05 to 0.24. Textiles used as personal clothing likely served as status markers among Wanka elites, but textile production too was broadly distributed among households (as indicated by spindle whorls and needles). Although the density of spindle whorls and needles was higher among elite households, this pattern was not strong and probably only reflected higher consumption rates. Production debris from metal was very low overall, suggesting that most metal was imported as finished objects from neighboring chiefdoms. Although manufacturing debris concentrated weakly in elite houses, no convincing evidence exists for attached specialization.

As a final consideration of Wanka households, little evidence exists for ritual and much of what we found was apparently household (versus group) based. No large ritual caches or other offerings were found. I have already discussed the remarkably limited amount of public ceremonial space, which was absent from all sites—except the center with its plazas that may have been part of a chiefly house group.

Small-scale household ritual practices were more common. Most important was burials below house floors. I take this to indicate house-based inheritance, a characteristic of house societies. This pattern of subfloor burials differs from other places in Peru where burial monuments or cemeteries were associated with community groups. Also found within households were special ritual deposits, including dog burials and small ritual offerings.

Elites were neither highly distinctive nor exclusive. The Wanka informants' description of independent households with chiefs, contingent on specific functions, was supported archaeologically. Chiefs were first among equals in a society that was evidently quite egalitarian in ethos, but dependent on leaders in war for defense and limited conquest. Elites did benefit—but only in limited ways—and were required to serve their communities.

THE BOTTOM LINE

Among chiefdoms the corporate mode of production most clearly characterizes chiefdoms with settlement hierarchies and extensive fortification, but with little structural inequality. Benefits of warrior chiefs' work are constrained by segmentary dynamics, within which their obligations are clear but their rights problematic. The primary function of the polity is to defend the corporate group's ownership of productive resources, which especially involves facilities that intensify agriculture. Communities are effectively tethered to these engineered landscapes. Hillforts are defensive, rather than ritual, as their primary organizational tool.

Ethnographically, we know these leaders to have been chiefs. For the Wanka and also the Polynesian Maori, although recognized by title and authority, leaders are not much distinguished symbolically; they are not visually separated from their communities, in which they maneuver to organize social labor to construct defenses, but giving up such authority when not required.

Such leaders probably engage in feasting associated with status competition and alliance building, but quite remarkably the amount of social labor funding rituals and building ritual structures is limited.

The Tunanmarca polity provides an example of the corporate mode of production associated with warfare. The rich ethnohistorical database works well to clarify archaeological evidence. This Andean example seems quite comparable organizationally to corporate mode of production cases from Iron Age Europe and the Pacific. Despite its size and three-tier settlement hierarchy, the organization of Tunanmarca households and communities appears to stand against a political hierarchy of power and authority. Although the central settlement is large, even city-like, it is internally anarchic without centralized planning (except for defensive walls). Ceremonialism is modest in the extreme and perhaps only associated with elite houses, which are minimally differentiated from others.

Chiefs rise to power through their services to the local population in defense. They work hard, risking their lives to defend the group, and their prestige is primarily defined by the security they delivered. Of course these leaders emphasize their essential roles and seek to expand their authority, but their ability to do so is constrained by little direct control of surplus mobilization and a strong anti-hierarchical cultural ethos.

ADDITIONAL READINGS

Arkush, Elizabeth, and Mark W. Allen (editors). 2006. *The Archaeology of Warfare: Prehistories of Raiding and Conflict*. Gainesville: University Press of Florida. This book describes the prehistory of raiding and conquest. Chapters consider several examples of warfare in chiefdoms, including Mark Allen on the Maori and Elsa Redmond and Charles Spencer on variation in warfare strategies.

Currás, Brais X., and Ines Sastre Prats (editors). 2020. *Alternative Iron Ages: Social Theory from Archaeological Analysis*. London: Routledge. Currás and Sastre's book considers the use of social theory for the archaeology of Iron Age Europe. Of particular importance are the chapters by Currás and Sastre on theories of egalitarianism, Bill Angelbeck on anarchist perspectives, and Niall Sharples on house society. This book shows the anti-hierarchy ethos of such hillfort societies in which leadership was problematic.

D'Altroy, Terence N., Christine A. Hastorf, and Associates. 2001. *Empire and Domestic Economy*. New York: Kluwer Academic. Compendium considering the Upper Mantaro Archaeological Research Project's (UMARP) study of Wanka society both before and after Inca imperial conquests. Chapters analyze settlement patterns (D'Altroy), architecture (DeMarrais), food remains (Hastorf and Sandefur), ceramics (Costin), wealth (Owen), and exchange (Earle).

Earle, Timothy. 2005. The Tunanmarca Polity of Highland Peru and Its Settlement System (AD 1350–1450). In *Settlement, Subsistence, and Social Complexity: Essays Honoring the Legacy of Jeffrey R. Parsons*, edited by Richard E. Blanton, pp. 89–118. Los Angeles: Cotsen Institute of Archaeology Press, University of California. This chapter summarizes evidence from UMARP for a single hillfort chiefdom that is the basis for this chapter. The previous book by D'Altroy and Hastorf provides additional details of these excavations and analyses.

Hastorf, Christine A., and Timothy Earle. 1985. Intensive Agriculture and the Geography of Political Change in the Upper Mantaro Region, Peru. In *Prehistoric Intensive Agriculture in the Tropics*, edited by I. S. Farrington, pp. 569–595. BAR International Series No. 232. Oxford, UK: Archaeopress. Working on UMARP, Hastorf and Earle summarize evidence for Wanka landesque capital, which included earthen-walled terraces, irrigation systems, drained fields, and ridged fields. Because of the relatively simple tasks involved in construction, they argue against a functional hypothesis that chiefs were required to organize labor to build intensive agricultural facilities.

Sastre, Inés. 2008. Community, Identity, and Conflict: Iron Age Warfare in the Iberian Northwest. *Current Anthropology* 49:1021–1051. Sastre argues that the Castro culture hillfort society was egalitarian (non-hierarchical) and organized to resist conquest and incorporation in regional polities. Each community is considered to have been small scale, economically self-sufficient, and politically independent. In combination with the Peruvian evidence, this article shows the spectrum represented by hillfort societies.

CHAPTER 6

ASIATIC MODE OF PRODUCTION: ENGINEERED LANDSCAPES

The Asiatic mode of production had high population densities supported by intensive agriculture over which chiefs could assert property rights and from which they could mobilize surplus. These overarching rights derived from elite investment in landscape construction (such as irrigation systems, terracing, and the like) and/or conquest of those facilities. Labor and staples were mobilized from commoner households in return for their rights to use these improved facilities. Such political economies were labor based and materialized by monuments.

During prehistory the emergence of social hierarchies relied foremost on mobilization of staples, especially food, but also items of everyday life such as clothing and pottery. Control of labor was maintained by the bottleneck of land ownership. But domination of subsistence, however, would have been difficult because staple commodity chains were short and organized primarily at the household level. Each household had the potential for broad subsistence independence.

OWNERSHIP OF ENGINEERED LANDSCAPES:
THE BOTTLENECK

The emergence of a landowning chiefly elite was in some ways an extension of what has been described previously, but in this model—an idealized form along a continuum of economic formations—chiefs rose to power by emphasizing rights (which were often divinely based) over commoner labor. Chiefly overlords granted commoners access to subsistence plots if the latter provided corvée labor and/or a portion of their staple produce. These were the densest chiefdoms and they were dependent on intensive subsistence, usually agricultural. As part of intensification, capital investments could include massive and extensive terracing, drainage, and irrigation.

Like feudal serfs, people were bound to their land and received subsistence allotments for which they were obligated to provide labor and staples to their lord. Commoners were circumscribed by high-density landscapes and the legal system of allotment; they had little mobility. Inter-polity warfare attempted to seize land and its facilities, but more importantly to appropriate the people's labor bound to the land. Successful conquering chiefs simply replaced previous overlords, as people stayed in place and gave labor and other surpluses to the new overlords.

Karl Marx defined the Asiatic (originally "Oriental") mode of production as characterizing agriculturally based political economies of Asian empires. He understood these eastern societies as segmentary in organization, whereby each independent community produced for its own needs and provided surpluses to imperial overlords. He saw them as remarkably non-dynamic, frozen in an agrarian past with simple divisions of labor unresponsive to the larger political dynamics seen in the West. He missed the (now well-recognized) fact that the stability of these agrarian states based on engineered landscapes represented sustainable economies with household and community management.

Surpluses derived from local commoner production and household labor gave communities bargaining power to check top-down autocracy. The flip side of community surpluses was the expectation that communities would receive specific services from elites—including large irrigation systems, regional peace, access to land, and elaborate religious ceremonies purported to guarantee divine support of community life.

The bargaining power of common farmers is highlighted by Marshall Sahlins's domestic mode of production with household self-sufficiency. Because commoner households managed the basic division of labor, no easy bottlenecks existed in the domestic mode of production and so channeling surpluses would seem to have been impractical. To develop a staple-based political economy required property systems in which household rights to resources were held by an elite sector.

The most elemental conditions of ownership in traditional societies were based on labor investment by households in productive facilities. Households produced the landesque capital and corporate or house property rights were represented by burial practices. But strong political economies based on subsistence did emerge and can be studied archaeologically. The creation of property rights provided bottlenecks allowing staple finance of chiefly institutions. Elemental household and community rights in land had to be abrogated or overlaid by new property regimes.

Processual Approaches to Engineered Landscapes

Prehistoric case examples of engineered landscapes abound from around the world. As recognized by Karl Wittfogel, a repeated association existed between irrigation and states societies. His hydraulic theory of the state was based on functionalism. Analogous to other highly sophistical technologies, he argued, large irrigation systems required specialized division of labor for engineering design, mobilization and direction of labor, reconstruction of facilities following flooding, and a plethora of other special activities. In simple terms, large irrigation required managerial oversight by chiefs and eventually state bureaucracies to provide the necessary expertise and capability.

Both Elman Service and Morton Fried used the hydraulic theory to help explain the formation of regional integration in chiefdoms, and the idea was broadly embraced by anthropologists. But many questions were raised about causality. For example, I propose that the real association of institutional complexity and irrigation (and by extension to other cases of engineered landscapes) involved instead how the facilities created bottlenecks in staple production. Archaeological examples of complex societies based on staple mobilization from irrigation are found independently—or largely independently—across the Middle East, Africa, China, Mesoamerica, Peru, the American Southwest, and the Pacific.

Middle Eastern Irrigation-Based Chiefdoms

The oldest agrarian chiefdoms and subsequent states have been documented archaeologically in the Middle East. Here we must consider briefly a possible typological contrast between chiefdoms and early city-states. Norman Yoffee, a formidable archaeologist and historian of the Middle East, argues that states developed sui generis and that chiefdoms were really an evolutionary side branch—a dead end actually—that did not underlay primary state formation. For him state formation is based on city-states that characterized early phases in the Middle Eastern and Aegean sequences.

Yoffe's argument, however, is really a typological conundrum—determining what to call the polities antecedent to states. In their thoughtful chapter looking at early Middle Eastern polities, Steven Falconer and Stephen Savage conclude that early "central places [in the Middle East] are frequently not cities and the entities themselves are not typically states" (2009, p. 131). My view is that the city-states found in the Middle East are best compared with chiefdoms based on the Asiatic mode of production. Let me explain.

Robert McC. Adams described how political systems in Mesopotamia had extensive irrigation systems, dense populations, settlement hierarchies, and political-religious institutions called temples. Population aggregations were considered "pre-urban," meaning that they were large permanent settlements but with little evidence for extensive internal craft specialization and markets. The overall size of polities was probably up to ten thousand, commonly associated with complex chiefdoms.

The extensive Copper Age Ubaid culture (6500–3800 BCE) illustrated such chiefdom-like polities. Settlement of this culture concentrated around the extensive Tigris and Euphrates rivers alluvial plain in southern Iraq. Gil Stein identifies this culture as composed of many local chiefdoms that varied in scale. Elites mobilized cereal staples and labor to support building central monument architecture and irrigation systems. Evidence of staple finance includes centralized storage facilities and accounting tokens for record keeping. Similar to chiefdoms described in Chapter 5, chiefs were not distinguished by wealth goods.

Individual Ubaid polities varied considerably in size, probably related to productivity of their irrigation complexes and other sources of power. They maintained central settlements with multiroom residential mud brick house complexes, centralized storage facilities, and monument architecture, but they had no enclosing defensive walls and craft specialization was apparently not attached to elite households.

Located in southern Iraq, the central settlement Eridu was about ten hectares in size. It governed a large polity with many small villages and hamlets. Eridu itself had a large central monument called a *ziggart* ("temple"); smaller settlements had no ceremonial or elite building. The economy involved staples from extensive irrigation systems and fairly minor external trade procured obsidian, copper, and other products.

Tell Abada is the most fully excavated Ubaid central place of the Fifth Millennium BCE (Figure 6.1). It is located on an alluvial plain along Iraq's eastern frontier (east of Baghdad and below the Zagros foothills). With 2–3 hectares of residential building complexes, the tell is a three-meter-tall hill created by continuous occupation over many generations. Complex A was a distinctive house complex, probably an elite compound. It was unusually large with three central halls and a distinctive patio perhaps for ceremonial events. Record-keeping tokens were found here. Complex I was also different, without a central hall but with space for animals and storage. Tell Abada was the central settlement for a fairly small Ubaid chiefdom based on staple finance, in which animals may well have been a wealth item. Craft specialization, however, appears not to have been attached to the special sectors of the site; the three ceramic kiln were broadly distributed.

Tells are artificial hills built up by trash accumulation during long occupations. Thus they represented strong residential associations with a particular place that I believe involved corporate ownership of land, probably associated with the house complexes. In the surrounding areas were smaller village sites (often less than one hectare) with commoner residences. These characteristics fit well within a comparative understanding of chiefdoms. The scale, settlement hierarchy, and religious institutional development of Ubaid society combined characteristics of ritual and corporate modalities. I believe

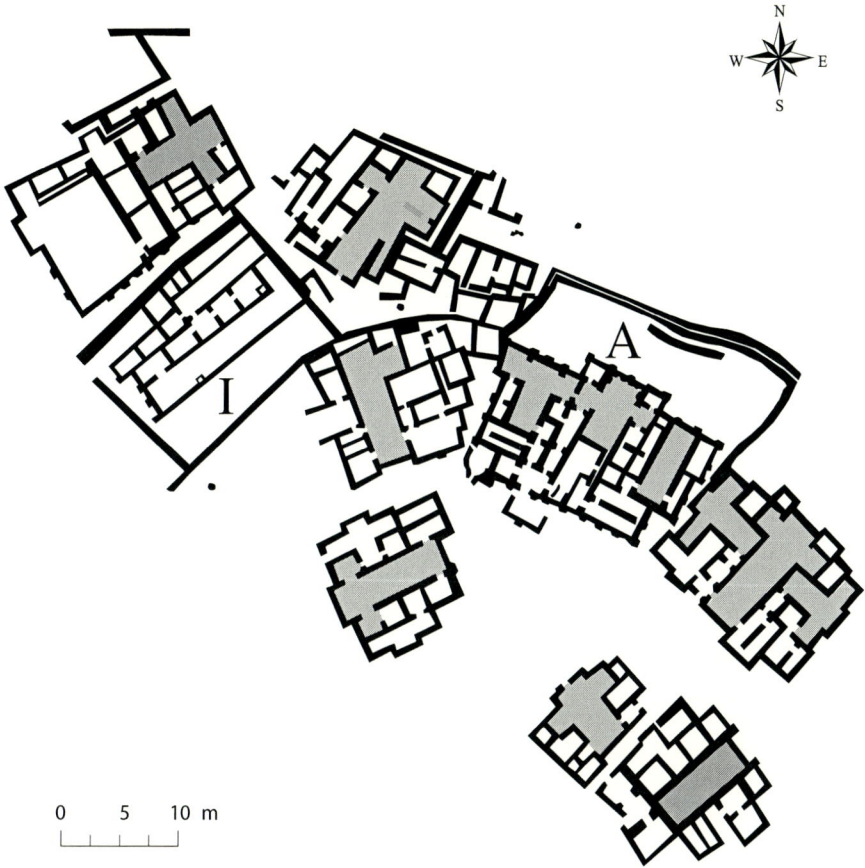

Figure 6.1. Tell Abada of the Ubaid Culture of Copper Age Mesopotamia. This tell contained a probable elite compound (A) and a storage-animal holding complex (I). Special rooms (halls) are shaded and the three isolated dots indicate ceramic kilns. Such centers included multiroomed mud brick house complexes and monumental buildings. Central places with associated settlement hierarchies organized regional populations at chiefdom scales. Illustration prepared by Jason Ur and modified by Mark Hauser.

these city-states were made possible by the construction of engineered landscapes that included irrigation systems needed to support (and circumscribe) a dense population in a dry environment.

The development of religiously based institutions for political integration created an identity for the polity since it allowed for staple mobilization, stored in the warehouses, that financed new political institutions. Critical were probably new property relationships in which leaders with instrumental religious roles could mobilize surpluses from the irrigation facilities that they built, defended, and eventually conquered. With surpluses they could support particular power strategies that involved temple ideologies and legitimized centralized power.

HAWAIIAN ISLAND COMPLEX CHIEFDOM–STATES

The history and prehistory of the Hawaiian Islands have been well documented during the last forty years. The National Science Foundation has supported major scientific projects focused on historical documents (especially land claims), archaeological survey, and substantial excavations. Perhaps the most influential work has been done by Marshall Sahlins and Patrick Kirch. The scope of survey and excavation has been expanded greatly by contract documentation funded by developers.

Polynesian mariners discovered and colonized the islands sometime after 800 CE. Over time these colonists formed political institutions that governed whole islands. By the time of first western contact in 1778 CE, Hawaiian society was the most centralized in the Pacific and provided a vivid example of the Asiatic mode of production as it supported the evolution of institutions of power. Subsistence depended on intensive agricultural facilities, especially irrigation systems for taro cultivation but also dryland terraces. Hawaiian chiefs came to form a distinctive landowning class that allocated farm plots to commoners in return for their labor.

Pristine archaic chiefdom-states on the Hawaiian Islands were a vivid example of primary social evolution of large-scale polities. Population growth, intensification of production, risk and sustainability, warfare, and property relationships created conditions for its political economy. The society was highly stratified with god-like ruling chiefs dressed elaborately, wearing cloaks and helmets adorned with rare and brilliant bird feathers and crafted by specialists attached to the chiefs to represent the clothing of gods (Figure 6.2).

Hawaiian Ethnohistory

As discussed by Patrick Kirch, although the Polynesians of Hawai'i were without writing, their history can be reliably established by combining ethnohistorical and archaeological material. At time of contact, western sources (including logs, diaries, letters, and reminiscences by explorers, traders, and early missionaries—many published to meet European eagerness to learn about people of the world) and Hawaiian oral histories documented a strongly stratified state-like society (see Chapter 2). Taught by early missionaries to write phonetically, Hawaiian authors described in their native language their traditional social organization, practices, religious ceremonies, oral histories, and myths.

Figure 6.2. Image of a Hawaiian chief dressed in feather cloak and helmet. The feathered crest over the helmet and across the back of the cloak (not shown) signified rainbows that identified the presence of a god. Illustration by John Webber.

During the nineteenth century, the Hawaiian state increasingly adopted western legal standards and other means of goverance. In what was called the Great Mahele, a new land tenure law asigned fee-simple ownership of plots and house lots to individual common farmers. To receive land the farmer had to describe how he had received and worked the land. Recorded in Hawaiian, these land records provide an invaluable trove of legal documents describing traditional land tenure practices. "Rescue" ethnographies by anthropologists

interviewing older native informants provide further understanding of traditional lifeways that were maintained into the twentieth century.

Western historical records began in 1778, when the British explorer Captain James Cook anchored off Waimea on the southern coast of Kaua'i. Cook's
illustrator John Webber captured daily life in the Waimea village, where walled
house lots were scattered across the valley floor and women are shown pound-
ing tapa cloth. He illustrated a stone temple nearby in Waimea, the home of
the gods represented by a cult house, standing god images, and an oracle tower
by which to communicate with the gods (Figure 6.3). The account described
extensive irrigation complexes up valley—where men worked the flooded taro
fields—and people eagerly trading food, feathers, and sexual services for novel
foreign goods, especially iron.

Hawaiian Domestic Economy

Based on both Hawaiian and western sources, economic organization in
Hawai'i depended on the farmstead. Families included a husband and wife

Figure 6.3. Hawaiian temple at Waimea, Kaua'i, at first contact (1778 CE). A cult house
(home of the gods) is to the left, standing god images (their earthly manifestations)
arranged in front, and the oracle tower behind where the temple priest communicated
with the gods. Illustration by John Webber.

living with natural and adopted children. A division of labor rendered men responsible for subsistence farming and fishing and corvée labor, and women responsible for childrearing, gathering, most household activities, and crafting of tapa cloth and woven mats. Children helped their parents. Informal adoption was essential to allow families to maintain independence by taking on or giving up children to balance labor needs within households. Because males were responsible for corvée labor, if a husband died a woman remarried quickly to retain rights to subsistence plots and access to community resources. Families were flexible production units fitting Sahlins's model of the domestic mode of production.

Traditionally, family rights to subsistence resources derived from chiefly allocations in return for corvée labor. Families received farm plots comprising irrigated pond fields for taro, an essential food. Additional crops included sweet potato, sugar cane, yams, and coconuts, which were grown on earthen divisions between pond fields and in dryland allocations. Farmers also raised pigs, letting them forage for themselves and feeding them sweet potatoes. Fish were raised in special ponds along the coast. Families also received a separate fenced lot, where their grass-and-frame houses stood close to irrigated plots and other resources they used.

Households operated largely independently but remained reliant on chiefs as landowners in a feudal-like system. This dependency created the bottleneck that channeled surpluses in labor and goods to support chiefs. This is the essence of the Asiatic mode of production. Elemental power was based on ownership of land and facilities, but commoners largely managed their daily labor with independence of action in a moral economy of assured subsistence.

Each household was part of a territorial community, typically a valley with its stream flowing from the central mountains. Knife-edged ridges marked territorial boundaries between communities. On geologically younger terrains, where erosion had not yet cut valleys, lines radiating from an island's center divided community territories vertically into pie segments. Each community was a self-supporting group of households with reciprocal arrangements and a chiefly land manager.

The paramount chief allocated each community as an income-producing estate to a community chief who was usually his close relative. Under each community chief was a manager, who put the commoners to work for the paramount chief. Each family had to farm allotments that produced food, and also work on public projects—including building irrigation and terracing systems, religious monuments, and fishponds. In return, chiefs provided access to productive subsistence facilities and support in times of hardship.

Hawaiian Surplus Mobilization

Surpluses provided resources to invest in the elemental sources of power that supported Hawaiian chiefdoms. The taro, sweet potatoes, and pigs from communities could be used by their chiefs to support a range of activities and people including construction of irrigated fields and fishponds; building of religious places; sponsorship of ceremonies; and patronage of land managers, warriors, craftsmen, and priests.

Economy

First were investments in the economic base. Surpluses supported construction of farming and fishing facilities, annual maintenance (such as cleaning ditches and reinforcing dams), and reconstruction required by occasional catastrophic loss due to flooding. Mobilization also sustained specialists attached to chiefs. Specialists were not involved in commodity production for exchange; rather, they made high-end items like feather capes for their patrons, weapons for warriors, and seaworthy canoes for pelagic fishing and war. Specialists received land in return for their support and may at times have been members of chiefly households.

Warfare

Second was investment in warfare. Wars were frequently mentioned in historical accounts as conditions of chiefly life and concern. Ruling chiefs sustained a cadre of warriors, highly trained and effective fighters. Warriors were attached as power specialists—defending the chief's authority and ownership rights, conquering new lands and their people, and punishing communities that did not provide sufficient tribute. Wars appear to have had little impact on commoners (who lived in unfortified, dispersed settlements) but a defeated chief lost all land and was likely killed to purge future rivalry. The outcome of wars for commoners was the replacement of community chiefs but with unchanged corvée obligations.

Success or failure in war determined the paramount chief's rule, his access to surpluses, and therefore his institutional power. Warfare was conquest based and most chiefs came to power by defeating rivals. Ownership of land, on which staple finance was grounded, was based on the physical taking of land with its farmers. This was thus a different form of warfare than described for the corporate mode of production (see Chapter 5), where fighting was primarily between communities for land. Of course these variants represented a continuum of goals.

Warfare existed historically among all Polynesian chiefdoms and certainly among all Hawaiian chiefdoms. It was most prevalent on Maui and the Big Island, where complex chiefdoms developed state-like structures through large-scale conquest and consolidation. Patrick Kirch argues that warfare was the primary mechanism for the creation of Hawaiian chiefdom-states. With lower population densities and dependent primarily on dryland farming rather than irrigation, warfare on the Big Island was necessary both to secure adequate surpluses and to offset the higher risks in surplus production inherent in dryland farming.

This makes the important point (discussed in Chapter 1) that control within chiefdoms at lower population densities was fundamentally different from that at higher densities. A comparative ethnographic study of African societies shows that political scale was inversely related to population density. At lower population densities, conquest warfare and a state-like social system appear to have been necessary.

Religion

Third was investment in ideology linked to ritual and religion. The gods of the Hawaiian Islands included several high gods, especially Lono responsible for land fertility and Ku responsible for success in war. The chiefs were lower gods on earth marked by distinctive dress, including feather cloaks and helmets that were decorated with overarching rainbows signifying the presence of gods. Many lesser spirits were associated with individual locations and high-risk activities like fishing.

All gods and spirits had associated ceremonies and rituals, often involving offerings and sacrifice. Most important were shrines, rituals, and priestly functionaries of the high gods. Much like agricultural facilities, chiefs mobilized resources and materials to construct and repeatedly reconstruct temples, supporting priests and underwriting rituals. Priests were power specialists attached to the high chiefs, much as land managers or warriors were tethered to their chief.

Two ceremonial cycles were significant. Primary was the annual *Makahiki* ceremony, in which an island's paramount chief—accompanied by his priests and warriors—traveled the coastal road around the island, stopping at each community's shrine to receive obligated "gifts." In this processional the high chief was the earthly manifestation of Lono, god of fertility of the land and its people. Gifts to Lono were carefully evaluated. Good offerings would guarantee productivity of the community in the coming year; inadequate gifts would be punished by the warriors escorting the high chief. These gifts were thus a tax collected within a ritual context.

Additionally, there were ceremonies housed at the large shrine dedicated to Ku. These were temples of the paramount chief, suggesting his primary role as defender of the chiefdom and conqueror of new territory. Such ceremonies were exceptionally sacred, involving human sacrifice—often of a defeated adversary.

Judging from historical records, political strategies of the high chiefs involved these three elemental powers. Fundamental was the subsistence economy for which commoners labored in their fields. Because communities were chiefly property, labor, food, and materials were mobilized to support institutional power. In a way chiefly power strategies could be presented as services to farmers, from whom the surpluses were mobilized—providing productive farms, protection in war, and exciting ceremonies. We know these conclusions from recorded history.

Hawaiian Archaeology

Archaeology has documented a diachronic evolution of Hawaiian chiefly institutions, especially as they involved engineering landscapes. Because of their physical permanency, irrigation ditches and terraces, territorial markers and roads, and religious monuments provide means to study labor mobilization and management.

We have already discussed labor invested for the construction of religious monuments (ritual mode of production) and defensive facilities (corporate mode of production). For the Asiatic mode of production, most important constructions were agricultural systems and facilities over which chiefs could assert property relations. The pristine Hawaiian chiefdom-states document how this linkage can be understood from a political economy perspective.

Archaeology has documented settlement patterns for Hawaiian chiefdoms. The elemental settlement feature is the house defined by a paved platform. These paved surfaces are typically scattered in the lower valleys close to primary farming and fishing grounds. Houses formed strings along the beaches, each house separated from the next. Houses did not cluster into villages and nothing approximating a town or urban settlement existed. The absence of a settlement hierarchy for Hawaiian prehistory is noteworthy, representing a rather distinctive pattern for chiefdoms.

We should step back to look at the Hawaiian chronology as it relates to the productive economy as a source of power based on food production and corresponding control over labor. Scattered across the Pacific, starting about 1000 BCE, remote island groupings were among the last places on earth to be colonized. Using ingenious sailing canoes, Polynesians explored, discovered, and settled virtually all inhabitable Pacific islands. Small colonizing groups expanded, subsistence production intensified, and a rather remarkable range of societies evolved. The outcome is a natural laboratory of historical experimentation, whereby some societies remained quite simple and almost egalitarian (for example, Tikopia described in Chapter 1), while archaic states developed on the Hawaiian Islands and Tonga.

Hawaiian Phases of Social Development

Phases of colonization, settlement, subsistence intensification, and social evolution on the Hawaiian Islands can be summarized as three steps.

Settling the Islands

Following initial colonization about 1000 CE, open land was available to all comers. Populations spread out along the coast, largely dependent on maritime resources and simple horticulture. Irrigation and drainage systems were practiced but only on limited scales. Settlements were small and scattered. Probably no enforceable landownership existed; people could move freely toward subsistence opportunities and away from chiefly demands. No landscape construction has been identified. Although probably retaining elements of chiefly structure common to all Polynesian societies, the primary mode of production was flexible and kin ordered with little or no surplus mobilization.

Forming Valley Polities

By about 1400 CE local valley-scale polities emerged in which land ownership was apparently held by individual lineages or "houses" (as described by Firth for Tikopia). Spreading along the coast and into the interior, the number of these small settlements increased. Clearing upland forests, however, accelerated erosion. As an unintended consequence, soil erosion enriched bottomland soils. Abandoning interior areas, populations concentrated near the coast and in valleys—where they were able to intensify subsistence production by constructing small irrigated systems, fishponds, tree groves of bananas, breadfruit, and coconut, as well as ritual monuments, pathways, and division walls. Although composed of small-scale systems, these irrigation zones were highly productive pockets over which ownership must have been defended.

At this time temples with stone platforms were built for religious structures that likely materialized group linkages to land. Local chiefs would have served to mobilize resources and labor to build these monuments and support festivals, and of course to defend the community land and its facilities. As described by Kirch, we can imagine somewhat different roles for warfare and chiefs related to the wet (irrigation-based valleys) and dry (farming in areas without streams to supply irrigation) corporate communities.

I suggest that new polities, in the hundreds or low thousands of people, would have represented a corporate mode of production. Based on homologous similarities to the Marquesas Islands (see Chapter 1), each valley or small cluster of valleys probably formed a separate local chiefdom. Land would have been corporately owned by local house groups and individual families would have held use rights to their plots. Warfare was probably ubiquitous between valley polities and chiefs would have assumed an important defensive function.

At first glance the lack of fortified facilities might have appeared counter to comparable chiefdoms, but natural valley ridges provided defenses against neighboring communities. In locations without eroded valleys or stream systems, however, irrigation was impossible and populations built dryland agricultural terraces. As another anomaly, probably an outcome of the low population density and natural defenses, inter-community warfare did not create corporate villages living within defensive walls.

Formation of Island-Wide Chiefdom-States

By about 1650 CE conquest warfare formed island-wide chiefdom-states. Ruling chiefs set out to subjugate broad swaths of territory that had originally been subdivided among separate valleys. Through conquest high chiefs abrogated ancient Polynesian lineage property rights and imposed a feudal-like system, in which commoners gave obligated labor to chiefs in return for access to former lineage land.

Engineered Landscapes at Time of First Contact

At first western contact, archaeology documents a remarkable engineered landscape across the islands. Most impressive were extensive irrigation com-

Figure 6.4. Photograph of a traditional Hawaiian irrigation system of taro pondfields that are still in use in Hanalei, Hawai'i.

plexes and dryland field terraces (Figure 6.4). Where stream systems had been established, almost every hectare of bottom alluvium and adjacent slopes was used for irrigation. These irrigation systems consisted of earthen ditches—sometimes supported by stonewalls—and side channels that watered clusters of terraced fields. They were terraced pondfields, each a separate flooded field in which wet taro was grown.

Terraces were typically reinforced with stone retaining walls, which remain visible archaeologically. Each pondfield was a separate terrace surrounded by raised earthen banks enclosing water-filled basins. The banks created space for paths and other crops. Taken during my fieldwork in Hanalei, Kaua'i, the photograph shows fields at different stages of growth from fallow to harvest; this staging allows for near continuous production. Taro is now grown primarily for market and used by Hawaiians as a staple and ceremonial dish (po'i) in the luau.

Taro fields stepped down the slope and water flowed from terrace to terrace through small channels cut in the earthen walls. The size of the terraces varied substantially, averaging from 40–400 square meters on individual irrigation systems. Larger terraces were found on alluvial floors and smaller terraces were found on edging slopes, in small valleys, and in the back of major valleys. Smaller taro fields would have been easier for families to manage individually, because of problems with scheduling crops and labor. The irrigation systems in the lower valley segments—with larger fields—were apparently the focus of chiefly management aimed at surplus mobilization.

Irrigation existed across the Hawaiian Islands but dominated the geologically older islands, including Kaua'i, Oahu, and western Maui. Many irrigation systems continued in use into the historic period, often converted to rice fields, and some continue to be used today for commercial taro production. Distributed unevenly across the islands, archaeological remains of irrigation concentrate in core zones with extensive bottom alluvium. Especially on the northern coasts of the islands, where the valleys were largest and most developed, taro fields stretched between valley walls to the sea. Often fishponds were constructed on coral reefs fringing the coast.

Although the extent of irrigation was impressive, the need for centralized management—contrary to what Karl Wittfogel had originally proposed—was minimal. Each valley was composed of many separate and quite small irrigation systems. On the north coast of Kaua'i, protohistoric irrigation systems averaged less than three (maximum of fourteen) hectares and were farmed by an average of six (maximum of fifty) families.

These small irrigation systems would easily have been constructed by family cooperation. With the Great Mahele, when farmers received rights to their own irrigation plots, one farmer remarked in legal documents, "We are our own land managers now"; and so they were through the historic period. Cross-culturally, systems of this scale did not require centralized management. Rather, chiefly management had served to mobilize surpluses.

Extensive dryland field systems were located on the western slopes of the Big Island and in eastern Maui, where no streams existed for irrigation. In a broad band at mid-elevation with adequate rainfall, terraced fields were developed for sweet potato and dryland taro. Each terrace cleared and leveled rough volcanic slopes, creating fields for permanent agriculture, but with higher risk and lower productivity than the irrigated taro pondfields elsewhere. Although nothing in the terraces would seem to have required centralized management, many were built rapidly—evidently under chiefly direction.

The built landscape thus defined both wet and dry farm plots. The intensified agricultural facilities were highly productive and relatively easy to dominate. Enforced by warriors, these facilities became bottlenecks in the staple economy. Conquest warfare seized these productive facilities and more appear to have been built under chiefly stewardship. Chiefs provided an essential service—developing productive, low-risk farmland—and in return received staples for political finance.

Auxiliary Ideological Power on the Hawaiian Islands

The evolution of the Hawaiian state appears to have depended on high population density, productive agricultural facilities, strong circumscription, and the resulting ability to assert ownership through conquest warfare. Such institutional ownership of intensified landscapes circumscribed populations that underlay the emergence of most early states worldwide, based on the Asiatic mode of production. The lack of an exit strategy for farmers limited their bargaining power; as described by Michael Mann, peasants were tied to their allocated land plots. But chiefly dependency on commoner labor pressured elites to serve their populations in order to overcome resistance.

Built facilities also linked to other sources of power. Most dominant archaeologically are the many religious shrines scattered across the islands. Each community had at least one permanent site for community ritual, which—consistent with the ritual mode of production—situated people in place. Of varying size and labor investment, these shrines were usually stone-built platforms (often surrounded by standing walls) on which were constructed sacred structures and wood figures: the earthly manifestations of the gods. Here community ceremonies took place, including—during the annual *Makahiki* ceremony—offerings to the paramount chief, the earthly manifestation of the fertility god Lono. Smaller shrines were dedicated to fishing gods and other spirits.

The construction of community temples dates to the second phase of the archaeological sequence, when community-based lineages are thought to have emerged. With the formation of island-wide chiefdoms, a hierarchy of temples materialized the political hierarchy of power.

Dominating the temple hierarchy, a few particularly large structures were constructed on Maui and Hawai'i. The latter was described historically as the temple of the war god Ku associated with the paramount chief of the island, whose polity was fashioned by warfare. Importantly, the scale of the religious monuments across the Hawaiian Islands is impressive, but actually modest when compared with some other chiefdoms (for example, in the American Southeast or the early chiefdom city-states of the Middle East; see Chapters 4 and 5). The role of ideological power in chiefdoms was quite variable.

Other physical markings of the Hawaiian landscape included walls that marked divisions of the communities into neighboring groups and trails that integrated communities from the mountains to the sea and linked them together. Trails surrounded the islands, linking all communities and forming the architecture for the annual *Makahiki* circulation by the paramount chief. Fortifications, however, were all but absent. Settlements were dispersed and small, nothing approaching a city or even a small town. This lack of concern with defense (no fortification) probably reflects the naturally defensive topography of valley ridges and the conquest objectives of war.

THE BOTTOM LINE

The historical record of the Hawaiian Island chiefdom-states documents highly stratified societies with god kings (paramount chiefs) who rule individual islands, each of which is composed of many valley-sized communities arranged in pie-like segments around the islands. Contact history and oral history provide rich documentation of this Asiatic mode of production based on high population densities, intensive agriculture, and staple finance to sustain institutional power. Chiefs own land that commoners use for their subsistence, and in return provide corvée labor to produce surpluses for the chiefs.

This model is similar to what probably exists for complex agrarian chiefdoms around the world, often manifested as city-states. The Hawaiian case, however, is unusual because of the severe circumscription of the islands, the isolation of the islands from world trade, the absence of markets, and no cities or even sizeable settlements. In return for surpluses, the chiefs provide key services to their populations—including productive irrigation systems, a safety net in disaster, and impressive ceremonies.

Archaeologically, physical landscape constructions provide permanent alterations. These capital improvements formalize political strategies. The irrigation systems create the intensive, sustainable, and productive economy

with the bottleneck of land ownership on which the staple-financed political economy is based. The engineering of fields, houses, religious shrines,
and trails carefully mark people-land relationships based on rights and responsibilities.

The political economy relies on chiefly ownership, permitted by the concentrated and productive nature of its agriculture. Many (if not most) chiefdoms outside the spheres of states and emergent world economies probably
rest on intensive agricultural production and systems of staple finance. This
pattern contrasts sharply to the pattern of low-density complexity that we
now consider closely linked with agrarian states through raiding, trade, and
ideology.

ADDITIONAL READINGS

Adams, Robert McC. 1966. *The Evolution of Urban Society: Early Mesopotamia and Prehispanic Mexico*. Chicago: Aldine. Adams compares the independent emergence of states in Mesopotamia and Mesoamerica. His
approach relies heavily on settlement pattern analyses to document the control exerted by an emergent hierarchy over the economy. Irrigation is critical
to his analysis, continuing a Marxist approach articulated by V. Gordon
Childe.

Cook, James. 1967. *The Journals of Captain James Cook on His Voyages of
Discovery, Vol. III: The Voyage of the Resolution and Discovery, 1776–1780*.
Edited by J. C. Beaglehole. Cambridge, UK: Cambridge University Press.
James Cook was a British naval officer and explorer in the Pacific. The journals of his voyages detail his discoveries and were quickly published to great
interest. They provide a first-hand account of the discovery of Hawaiian societies, which had developed independently of world systems.

Earle, Timothy. 1978. *Economic and Social Organization of a Complex Chiefdom: The Halelea District, Kaua'i, Hawaii*. Anthropological Papers No. 63,
Museum of Anthropology, University of Michigan, Ann Arbor. Based on my
doctoral dissertation, this monograph presents early research showing inad-
equacies of functionalist theories emphasizing prime movers (irrigation, trade,
and warfare) in the evolution of Hawaiian chiefdoms.

Earle, Timothy, and David Doyle. 2008. The Engineered Landscapes of Irrigation. In *Economics and the Transformation of Landscape*, edited by Lisa
Cliggett and Christopher A. Pool, pp.19–46. Lanham, MD: AltaMira Press.
From a keynote address, this chapter compares the development of complex
chiefdoms on the Hawaiian Islands with the American Southwest, where ir-

rigation was also important to the emergence of political complexity. The role of engineered landscapes and resulting property relationships is emphasized.

Falconer, Steven E., and Charles L. Redman (editors). 2009. *Polities and Power: Archaeological Perspectives on the Landscapes of Early States*. Tucson: University of Arizona Press. This edited book compares the city-states along the Levant at the edge of Mesopotamia. Chapters describe the human landscape of these chiefdom-scale early polities. The chapter by Falconer and Stephen Savage is particularly useful.

Handy, E. S. Craighill. 1940. *The Hawaiian Planter, Vol. 1*. Bulletin No. 161, Bernice Pauahi Bishop Museum, Honolulu. Handy's monograph describes traditional practices of taro agriculture. It is based on interviews with elderly Hawaiian farmers and limited descriptions of the historic spread of irrigation systems through the islands.

Kirch, Patrick V. 1994. *The Wet and the Dry: Irrigation and Agricultural Intensification in Polynesia*. Chicago: University of Chicago Press. Kirch is presently the leading Polynesian prehistorian, with extensive archaeological work across Pacific archipelagoes (including Hawai'i, Marquesas, Rapa Nui, and Tikopia). Based on his early work, this book draws connections between warfare and Polynesian chiefly expansion.

Kirch, Patrick V. 2010. *How Chiefs Became Kings: Divine Kingship and the Rise of Archaic States in Ancient Hawai'i*. Berkeley: University of California Press. Kirch describes the ethnohistorical and archaeological evidence for the emergence of divine kingship and the rise of archaic states in ancient Hawai'i.

Ladefoged, Thegn N., and Michael W. Graves. 2008. Variable Development of Dryland Agriculture in Hawai'i: A Fine-Grained Chronology from the Kohala Field System, Hawai'I Island. *Current Anthropology* 49:771–802. Ladefoged and Graves are processual archaeologists with extensive experience in Hawaiian prehistory. Ladefoged's research on dryland agriculture on the Big Island of Hawai'I provided the evidence for Kirch's view that downplayed the significance of irrigation in Polynesian political evolution.

Wittfogel, Karl. 1957. *Oriental Despotism: A Comparative Study of Total Power*. New Haven, CT: Yale University Press. The classic theoretical presentation of the hydraulic hypothesis for the evolution of states. Essentially, requirements of construction and maintenance of irrigation were thought to require centralized management by state bureaucracies. The book provides a cross-cultural description of the close association between archaic states and irrigation.

Yoffee, Norman. 1993. Too Many Chiefs? Or Safe Texts for the '90s. In *Ar-chaeological Theory: Who Sets the Agenda?* edited by Norman Yoffee and An-drew Sherratt, pp. 60–78. New York: Cambridge University Press. Yoffee presents a strong critique of chiefdoms as an evolutionary typology in the staged development of state societies. He believes that the antecedent for states were the city-states that characterized early Mesopotamia. Rather, he argues that chiefdoms were an aberrant social formation.

CHAPTER 7

PREDATORY MODE OF PRODUCTION AND WEALTH FINANCE

A t low population densities, the predatory mode of production was based on control over wealth circulation. These modalities have been called prestige goods economies, emphasizing channeled flows and distribution of high-end objects—including items denoting personal status or office, weapons, and ritual paraphernalia.

These communities were typically segmentary or house societies in which family groups could largely determine their own destiny by controlling their means of livelihood. If a chief became too demanding, families could simply move away. Although it seems incongruous that centralized leadership could form in maritime and pastoral societies, it often did occur linked to emergent world economies. Political economies could support chiefly power by channeling prestige goods, weapons, and slaves. By controlling these high-value and transferable objects, leaders established chieftaincies that merged dispersed groups to create chiefdom-scaled political institutions. Key was the attraction created by the special objects.

CONTROL OF WEALTH FLOWS

The question is how wealth flows were controlled by chiefs. This was done by a chief's ability in some situations to create bottlenecks. To understand bottlenecks here shifts property rights away from ownership of agricultural land per se and toward technologies and locations of trade. In these contexts special objects bound people to their chiefs through gift exchanges.

On the peripheries of urban states, ownership of boats (often seaworthy) or transport animals (horses, camels, and donkeys) typically provided bottlenecks for entrepreneurial raiding and trading; alternatively, in-place ownership (and defense) of trading pathways like rivers, passes, oases, or harbors allowed chiefs to extract portions of goods passing under their forts. Both bottlenecks depended on warrior might in raiding, protecting moving goods, and/or defending trading nodes. Chiefs held a special status as exalted warriors, akin to their role as defenders of community land.

Wealth-based chiefdoms depended on status distinctions linked to circulating prestige objects. Archaeologically, the markers of chiefs operating within the predatory mode of production contrasted sharply with other chiefly modes of production. Rather than the importance of monument construction, the possession of special objects (for example, those found in burials) defined individual distinctiveness. These political societies were highly variable, ranging from relatively small-scale chieftaincies of northern or central Europe to expansive pastoral empires of central Asia. Because these modes were linked to world economies, they especially characterized the Old World at the margins of urban states. But they also existed, to a more limited extent, in the New World—as described historically for Panamanian chiefdoms (see Chapter 1).

Understanding the predatory mode of production is based on Marx and Engel's vague notion of the Germanic mode of production. In line with European thinking of their time, the "democratic" Germanic mode of production was conceptualized in contrast to totalitarian Asiatic modes of production. In the Germanic mode, the political economy was thought to be based on independent farms organized intermittently by chieftains for defense and dispute resolution. Antonio Gilman summarizes its characteristics as consisting of autonomous households forming independent production units embedded within tribal groups. Leadership was weak but with a hereditary basis for authority.

The Scandinavian dispersed settlements systems of Bronze Age Europe fit this model well. Such societies had elements described as anarchistic. It also has much in common with the recent conception of house societies used to analyze the Austronesians of the Pacific and island Southeast Asia, the Vikings of Iceland, and American Northwest Coast societies. Elementarily, these societies were organized as independent social units embedded within fragile political institutions. They were stratified but weakly centralized based on differential ownership of key resources—what Morton Fried called stratified pre-state societies.

Such societies could have been transformed into regional chiefdoms by controlling wealth circulation. Chiefs drew independent households into regional chieftaincies by creating a distinguished warrior class marked by special objects. Using weapons and wealth as symbols of power and distinction, chiefs extracted and gifted the binding media of these status objects. This modality often was based on the high mobility seen in both pastoral and maritime economies, in which raiding of commodity flows has in pre-modern times been called piracy. A common characteristic appears to have been seizure and trade of slaves as labor, demanded especially within urban states.

SCANDINAVIAN CHIEFDOMS OF THE VIKING
AND BRONZE AGES

As a special case of the predatory mode of production, maritime chiefdoms—exemplified by the Viking and Bronze Age societies of northern Europe—illustrate the maritime mode of production described by Johan Ling, Kristian Kristiansen, and me. Engaging in international trade in metals, textiles, slaves, and exotics, Bronze Age warriors of Scandinavia achieved dominant, partly independent positions in society, allowing expansive chieftaincies and chiefly confederacies to form. Concurrently, such warrior fraternities were always disruptive, fragmenting political relationships as they sought personal distinction. The maritime mode of production model incorporates both centripetal and centrifugal forces associated with the world system of trade and political relationships that emerged across Eurasia at this time.

With deep roots in the Neolithic, the Scandinavian maritime economy was linked to a strong agro-pastoral section in which individuals raided for animals. I believe the particular economic mode that characterized the Bronze Age subsequently strengthened Viking social formation. To construct the model for the maritime mode of production, we begin with a historical summary of the Viking Age and its rich documentary sources. Then for the Bronze Age we look at the archaeological evidence for Scandinavia, building a model for the emergence of this economic modality.

The Viking Age: Historic Overview

Viking society is emblematic of a fierce, untamed northern Europe. Aggressiveness was signaled by warrior dress and weaponry and by wealth obtained in raiding and chiefly service. But Vikings were also free farmers, tied to their land across generations, and some were among Europe's most famous poets. Boats and farms constituted two basic house-like units. Each unit operated within a segmentary system, combining or dividing according to component personal interests. Although inherently decentralized, regionally stratified chieftainships maintained a hereditary aristocracy, celebrated warriors, free farmers, and slaves. Personal initiative, voyaging, surplus extraction, and flows of wealth created balancing forces of decentralization and hierarchy.

Independent Farmsteads

Concordant with the Germanic mode, farms were the primary productive units—the basal units of Scandinavian society. Douglas Bolender describes the individual Icelandic Viking farmstead as representing a house society organization—meaning that each farm retained relative subsistence autonomy, inherited rights to land materialized by burial of ancestors on the farm, and social inequality formed with unequal farm sizes. Viking house structures ranged considerably in their roofed area, and the wood framing of more affluent houses was elaborately carved with intricate and beautiful animal and mythical motifs.

Placement of a farm in the social hierarchy was easy, much as is possible when driving through a modern city. Landless people lived in rude hovels, free farmers inhabited moderate homes, and chieftains dwelt in large halls sufficient to entertain guests and supporters. Chiefly farms held fertile land worked by slaves and other attached labor to produce surpluses that attracted warriors and craftsmen. By building networks of personal support among kinsmen and others, chiefs formed political support across a microregion.

To seize metals and slaves, agricultural surpluses from chiefly farms financed maritime ventures. Arab, Frankish, and English accounts pictured Vikings as raiders enticed by precious metals, primarily silver. About 800,000 silver coins have been found in Scandinavia, more in fact than have been recovered in the regions of their origin (Figure 7.1). Such wealth was then gifted by chiefs to attract warriors and establish confederacies.

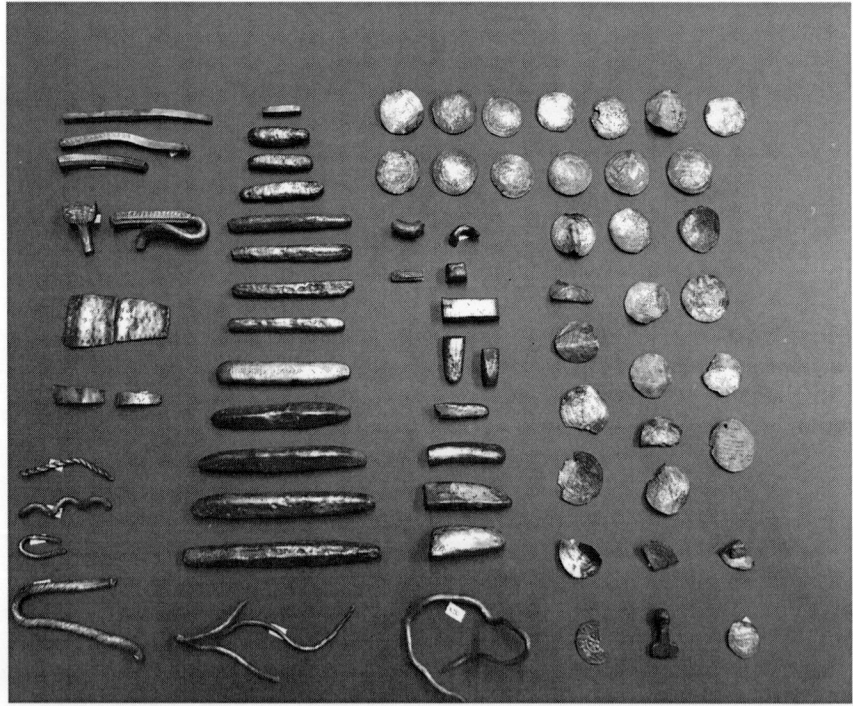

Figure 7.1. Viking silver hoard (about 1000 CE) from Ejstrup, Denmark, including thirty dirhems (Islamic coinage), two German coins, various ingots (likely from melted coins), some scrap, and one Thor's hammer. Such hoards probably represent plunder from systematic raiding and trading. Photo by Inge Kjaer Kristiansen, Museum Salling Archaeology, Skiva, Denmark.

Toward the end of the Viking Age, powerful chiefs assembled fleets and armies to expand their kingdoms by conquest and colonization—ruling for a time parts of Scandinavia, Iceland, England, Ireland, France, and beyond. State societies eventually built an overlay of forts, coastal market towns, and newly established Christian parish churches and cathedrals.

Maritime Trading and Raiding

Wealth from raiding and associated trading financed boat building and distant travels in search of wealth, conquest, and colonization. Although it is possible—and even likely—that non-chiefs could build boats and man crews, the logistical difficulties offered an advantage to chieftains to finance boat building and voyaging, and boat-owning chiefs benefited from voyages to amass wealth as political currency. Large chiefly longboats were capable of rapid and distant sea and riverine travel using oars and sails. These ships were built with a keel, overlapping planks, and upward projecting stern and bow that were carved with mythical beasts. Thirty or more meters in length, a chief's boat would lead a flotilla of smaller boats and crews attracted by potential rewards of raiding-trading voyages.

Concentrated to the north in Sweden and Norway, the maritime sector provided forest timber, skilled woodworkers, and sea-trained mariners. Estimating the requirements of shipbuilding, experimental archaeology has shown that a 30-meter-long seagoing craft required mobilization of a substantial workforce, something on the order of a hundred people working for a year. Boat building was complicated and expensive, involving cutting and moving large trees for boat timbers and compensating specialists working the wood and other materials (including wool and tar for sails). These tasks required careful coordination.

In addition, taking the boat to sea for four months meant that perhaps seventy men were lured from their farms and had to be fed and rewarded with shares and chiefly largesse. The cost of financing large boat building and voyaging was high and only chieftains could be major players in this political economy game.

To realize groups for boat building and long-distance raiding and trading, labor had to be transferred from fieldwork to voyaging. As described by historical documents, slaves apparently filled labor gaps by working on farms. Their labor (with different classifications) included heavy fieldwork, herding cattle, household chores, and farm management. With slave labor, free farmer-warriors could have set out to raise personal social standing and capital, as well as those of their chieftains. Although Scandinavian slaves did not occur in large numbers on ordinary farms, chiefly farms possessed more. Importantly, women were not warriors but they held high status, remaining on the farm to manage all activities.

As significant commodities, slaves were sought by Vikings both for domestic use and for international trade. Wherever Vikings moved in western

Europe, the Baltic, or Slavic regions, they captured people to sell as slaves. At their trading centers, Vikings sold slaves for the gold, silver, bronze, and other precious commodities described in Old Norse sources. As succinctly described by Price, raiding is slaving is trading.

Because chieftains owned many boats, flows of slaves, metals, and weapons were channeled disproportionately through their hands. With these wealth items chiefs could build their networks of support by distributing commodities to mark social status, arm warriors, and provide tools for craftsmen. Kings, aristocrats, and chieftains maintained specialists for working with precious metals, textiles, and other status objects for their own consumption and for special gifts. Ultimately, specialty manufacture occurred in towns under the control of kings, but local chieftains also supported craft production. This showed that the political economy was quite decentralized and allowed would-be chieftains to seek power and prestige.

In sum, Viking chiefdoms were segmentary polities, able to construct power networks through accumulating wealth and exchanging gifts. Terrestrial and maritime sectors held distinct but complementary potentials and skills to integrate a macroregional economy. In the land-based sector, all farms used slaves to provide labor. Larger and more productive chiefly farms could accumulate slave and servant labor to produce surpluses that supported warriors, artisans, and ritual specialists and funded construction and manning of boats and crews. Chiefly farms provided surpluses that could be invested especially in the maritime sector. This maritime mode of production, scholars believe, had ancestral roots in Scandinavian prehistory reaching back to the Bronze Age.

The Early Bronze Age of Scandinavia: Archaeological Evidence

The Scandinavian Bronze Age documents the formation of the maritime mode of production in Thy and Tanum, two regions of Scandinavia that Ling, Kristiansen, and I argue were linked in a chiefly confederacy. At this time long-distance trade (especially in metal) had emerged across Eurasia, creating a new world order as communities became dependent on metal supplies from distant places. With international interdependence the Bronze Age marked a significant economic revolution; new economic conditions supported a 50% population increase across Europe. Located to the far north, Scandinavia might seem to have been a frontier zone, but nothing could be further from the truth. A remarkable society developed there with concentrated metal wealth, large chiefly farms, and an impressive burial landscape.

To understand Bronze Age Nordic chiefdoms, I step back to summarize their historical antecedents. In Chapter 4 we considered the Early Neolithic during the third millennium (4000–3000 BCE). In the second millennium (3000–2000 BCE), these Early Neolithic communities were largely swept away by expanding peoples holding a distinctive cultural assemblage—corded ware pottery, new weapons, and often single burials under earthen mounds. Recent DNA data demonstrate that these people were migrants from the steppes with a pastoral economy. They appear to have largely exterminated the existing people.

In Scandinavia the new culture is defined by battle-axes (typically included with single male burials under an earthen barrow) and female burials with local amber jewelry. Almost no residences are known and houses were evidently fairly temporary, suggesting mobility. The pollen record at this time documents a rapid clearing of the forests by fire, apparently to establish grasslands for animals. We imagine this new society as comparable to the segmentary Nuer (see Chapter 1). Males were probably warriors raiding for animals to establish status and were responsible for defense of their social segment against outsiders.

A sea change occurred in Scandinavia around 2000 BCE, in what has been called the Dagger period. Most distinctive was a new weapon, the carefully crafted flint dagger that had both status value and killing capability (Figure 7.2). The daggers found in warrior burials were extraordinary—knapped by highly skilled specialists able to create the decorative long, parallel flaking. Additional changes included substantial amounts of metal obtained from distances, the abandoned use of local amber to mark status, and the formation of a farmhouse tradition. This period is connected with the Bell–Beaker phenomenon that represents migrations along the rivers and coasts of Europe, development of metal technology involving pyrotechnic specialists, establishment of international trade with a new boat technology, and a tradition of dispersed farmsteads (as associated with the Germanic mode of production).

The subsequent Early Bronze Age (1500–1100 BCE) realized the maritime mode of production with single farms, burial mounds placed high on the hills above farms, a hierarchy in size of houses and burial mounds, and an impressive concentration of metal wealth in some burials and caches. The economy was a mixed agro-pastoralism supporting a fairly low population density, perhaps one farm per square kilometer. Associated burial mounds suggested that ownership of land was house based, with independent farms inherited across generations.

Ling, Kristiansen, and I argue that the transformation in the political economy involved local intensification by chiefly farms, which financed improvements in seagoing boats and a network of economic facilitators (traders) and predators (raiders). The result was a new economic configuration with associated political changes. Though Scandinavian longhouses, burial mounds, and metal wealth document one archaeological culture, locally specific linkages to the political economy created different bottlenecks that selected for quite distinctive political formations.

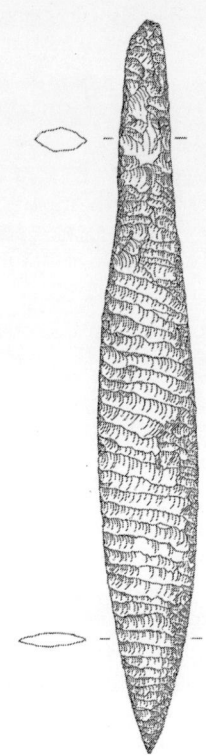

Figure 7.2. Carefully crafted flint dagger from a burial in Visby, Thy. Such daggers were manufactured in southern Scandinavia and traded widely, especially to the north where high-quality flint was unavailable. Illustration prepared by Beth Møller, Thisted Museum, for the Thy Archaeological Project.

We base our argument on archaeological research in two complementary areas—Thy in southern Scandinavia, with its extraordinary density of barrows and concentrated wealth; and Tanum in northern Scandinavia, with its richness of rock art and relative paucity of metal wealth (Figure 7.3). These areas were probably linked by chiefly confederacies.

The Early Bronze Age of the South: Thy, Denmark

Thy characterizes the agricultural richness of southern Scandinavia that includes the peninsulas of Jutland (extending north from Germany into the North Sea), Scania (extending south from Sweden into the Baltic), and many islands in between. This region became the medieval kingdom of Denmark—

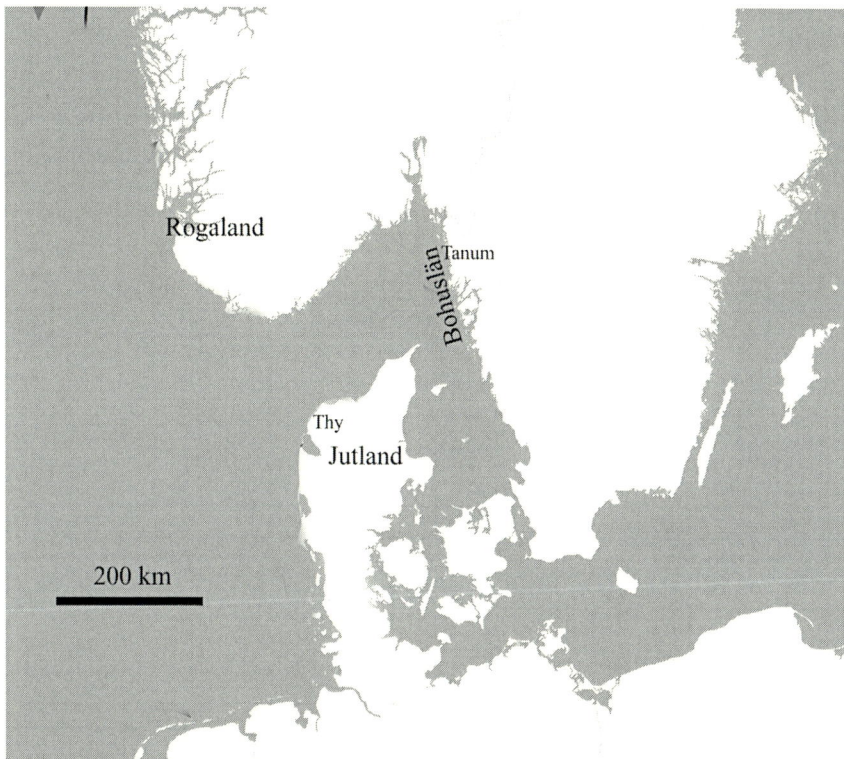

Figure 7.3. Map of southern Scandinavia showing the location of Thy on the glacial soils of Jutland, Denmark, and Tanum on the rocky west coast of Sweden. Illustration provided by Johan Ling.

a glacial landscape of low rolling hills, moraines, outwash plains, uplifted sea floors, sea-eroded cliffs, and sand spits.

Surplus Production in Farming

During the Bronze Age, the primary subsistence strategy in Thy was agro-pastoralism. The light sandy soils were ideal for cattle pasturage and cereal cultivation. At this time the heavier clay soils were avoided because they required more intensive farming methods. Farms were located on the lighter soils and coasts were never distant. Although maritime resources were rare in subsistence remains, maritime activities were highly likely.

Along the coasts, especially in Thy, amber washes up regularly after storms. Isolated outcrops of limestone were also an important source of flint, used by craftsmen to knap elaborate daggers (continuous from the Dagger period) and sturdy sickles. Amber, flint tools, and probably cattle hides were Thy's exports. The amber served throughout Europe as a wealth item, the flint daggers were a substitute for bronze weapons especially early in the period and to the north, and the sickles served broadly for agricultural intensification.

Central to the farm was a three-aisle longhouse. Most longhouses were about eighteen meters long and eight meters wide, with a double line of substantial posts supporting the roof and lighter posts framing wattle-and-daub walls. Some houses were significantly larger. Although no towns and villages existed, variation in farmhouses reflected social stratification—chiefly halls, free farmer and warrior residences, and poorer households probably of servants and slaves. The Thy Project excavated two chieftain halls that were over thirty meters long and constructed of massive roof-supporting posts and planked walls. These impressive buildings surely had the specialist carvings known for the Viking halls.

Contrasting with the association between other chiefly economic modalities and dramatically engineered landscapes, in Scandinavia the built environment was little evident. The primary improvements in staple production appear to have been clearing forests for pasturelands, plowing, and spreading household trash to improve soil fertility. No defensive works have been identified in Thy. Ritual structures—except for mortuary mounds—were smallscale structures, probably for family rituals. The built landscape included only farmhouses and matching burial mounds.

Building large halls and prominent burial monuments required substantial labor, and researchers believe successful farms became seats for chieftains managing surpluses. On low hills above the farms in Thy, there were several thousand barrows—earthen mounds over the graves of chieftains, warriors, and free farmers. Most were 2–3 meters tall and 15–20 meters in diameter, while a few large barrows were above five meters tall and stood prominently in the landscape.

A Warrior Elite

A warrior ethos was distinctive to the Nordic Bronze Age. This warrior tradition was a direct continuity from the Battle Axe and Dagger period cultures. Weapons, including bronze swords and daggers and less commonly axes, arrow points, and spears, were routinely included with single burials or caches. These must have been personal weapons of trained warriors.

Nordic society had a warrior aristocracy—a few chiefs with highly elaborate swords used for dress and warriors and free farmers with fighting swords showing extensive damage and resharpening. Perhaps unexpectedly, the presence of this weaponry was found with no evidence of defensive works. I interpret this pattern to show that warriors were involved primarily in raiding at a distance, rather than local defense of territory (see Chapter 4).

During the Bronze Age throughout Europe, Scandinavia was among the richest regions for metal wealth. Other wealth included woolen textiles and a range of distinctive objects, seen most clearly in the oak casket burials where preservation was almost complete. Regionally, these valuables were concentrated in southern areas, especially Jutland and then the islands. The singularity in metal richness included Thy—our research area on the northwest coast of Jutland—where bronze objects, dated stylistically to Period III (1300–1100 BCE), document dramatic increase in both flange-hilted (warrior) swords and full-hilted (chiefly) swords.

The high frequency of bronze swords records the warrior ethos of Bronze Age Scandinavian society. They apparently were placed in the burial mounds of every free farmer and warrior. Only a fraction (perhaps 20%) of the population was buried in earthen mounds, apparently those owning farms. Associated with the unequal labor investments in houses and burial mounds, a few chieftains controlled the bulk of riches.

Importance of Distant Trading

These riches were primarily long-distance imports. No Scandinavian metal wealth derived from local ores, although most of the objects were locally manufactured (probably by attached specialists). Lead isotope analyses of Early Bronze Age Scandinavian metals from Thy document that all bronze was made from imported metal, mostly transmitted by an Atlantic trade network. On Jutland's coast Thy held a favorable position as a transit zone for metals coming by boat. Seaways, facilitated by ocean currents, apparently existed from the British Isles to Jutland and in turn to western Sweden and southeastern Norway.

Until modern times fishermen used these currents to save time and effort and Bronze Age mariners would have benefited from them. But what is the archaeological documentation for seagoing boats? Nothing is available from Jutland, or from southern Scandinavia more generally, where agricultural intensification during the Bronze Age exhausted timber suitable for boat construction. We must look north, where different resources created a complementary maritime-based world of chieftains.

The key question remains, however. How did the Bronze Age chieftains of Thy and Scandinavia more generally accumulate quantities of imported metal and other wealth on the fringe of Europe? Here the archaeological evidence remains thin, and the role of modeling becomes critical to establish conditions that could have created advantages in trade compared with the rest of Europe.

The Early Bronze Age of the North: Tanum, Sweden

Tanum is a coastal district in western Sweden where rocky shores, bays, and small valleys supported a mixed maritime-agricultural economy. During the Bronze Age, sea level was higher than today and many embayments provided good harbors. In back of the coasts, forested mountains rose steeply out of the sea. This zone has long been important for timber and wild game was plentiful. From 1500 to 1000 BCE, population densities were low—probably less than a farm per two square kilometers. Proximity to the sea and good timber for boats made maritime subsistence resources important.

Culturally, the Bronze Age pattern in Tanum was typical: independent farmsteads, associated burial mounds with some wealth, often flint daggers, and more rarely bronze tools and decorative items. The Early Bronze Age cultural pattern points to frequent interregional interaction. Along Sweden's rocky coast, large rock cairn burial mounds were located above harbors, suggesting chiefly ownership of these nodes. This pattern is in sharp contrast to the chiefly burial mounds in the south associated with agro-pastoral soils.

A broad interaction sphere must have existed among Denmark, Sweden, and Norway involving the movement of both people and their social structure. Several key raw materials were lacking in the north and the region was dependent on trade for metal, flint, and probably cattle and hides. Amber was not available on these coasts. What could they offer to trade for imported commodities from the south?

Boats of the North

The Tanum people had access to the seaworthy crafts illustrated by its world-famous Bronze Age rock art. About 70% of the rock art in Tanum was located proximate to a large bay. Impressive panels depict warriors and chieftains armed with bronze weapons found in burials in Thy, but which were rare or nonexistent in the region's burials.

Nearly two thousand images of boats have been documented in Tanum. Seagoing crafts had a shape remarkably similar to early Iron Age boats and also no sails. Boats were depicted with a sweeping line of a keel and parallel upturned stems at bow and stern. They were apparently propelled by paddlers, indicated in the art by upright lines. Boats varied considerably in length and crew size. Many were quite small with eight or so crew members, while a few had 25 or more crew members—some differentiated as chiefs, warriors, and/or ritual specialists. These boats were evidently able to carry warriors across seas or along rivers for distant raiding. In Figure 7.4 warriors are shown with their battle gear (axes, swords worn at the waist, shields, spears, and bows). These bronze weapons were rare or nonexistent in Tanum, but common in Thy.

Direct evidence of these boats dates to descendant groups in the Iron Age around 375 BCE. From a bog on the southern Danish island of Als, the well-

Figure 7.4. Rock art image from Tanum, Sweden, showing boats and warriors from the Bronze Age. An effective boat technology allowed Scandinavian chieftains to concentrate the flow of wealth and create class-based warrior societies (as illustrated in the rock art). Illustration provided by Johan Ling, Director, Rock Art Research Archive, Tanum.

preserved Hjortspring boat is a dead ringer for Bronze Age images, documenting a continuous-plank boat-building tradition. Apparently a votive offering, the boat was loaded with weaponry. It was about twenty meters long, constructed with a keel, planks, and double stems at bow and stern. A line of thwarts served as benches for paddlers. A Hjortspring replica shows that such boats would have weighed just over five hundred kilos. They were capable of carrying 24 men and their weapons rapidly for considerable distances on the high seas, and would have been ideal for distant raiding and trading.

Experimental studies show substantial labor and timber requirements for Tanum-like boat construction. Such a boat would have needed about 6,500 person hours to build. These war canoes were similar to those of the Solomon Islands (see below) in requiring years for construction. Financed by chiefs, as in the Oceanic cases, a boat would likely have been the chief's property.

Abundant ship images in Tanum undoubtedly represented local practices for building and manning boats, which became a specialized activity in the macroregional division of labor of Bronze Age Scandinavia. According to

Ling, this rock art probably showed individual agency by mariners as they created rituals for success in managing risky, long-distance expeditions.

The Maritime Sector

The formation of a maritime sector in Scandinavia—as illustrated by Tanum—would have included coastal people using boats for everyday life (fishing, marine mammal hunting, socializing, and trade). Special maritime skills included boat building and crewing, but perhaps most significantly skills in woodworking so important for constructing reliable water craft. Here the close proximity of mature forest stands would have been essential for high-quality lumber. By at least 1300 BCE, the forests in southern Scandinavia were depleted by clearing for pasturage, fuel, and house construction. People of Thy were making do with poor-quality lumber. Good wood and skilled craftsmen to construct impressive chiefly halls would likely have come from the north or specially managed local forests.

For the political economy, the wood and woodworking skills for the seaworthy ships were most probably the basis for obtaining metal wealth in southern Scandinavia. Historical documents from the twelfth century CE record that coastal Sweden traded timber and boats for agro-pastoral products from Jutland, and during historical times the Danish naval fleet was constructed with timber from Tanum.

MODELING CHIEFLY CONFEDERACIES
IN BRONZE AGE SCANDINAVIA

A Scandinavian model of transregional chiefly confederacies suggests a reasonable way to explain the observed pattern of complementary relationships between two sectors—an agricultural sector in southern Scandinavia capable of producing staple surpluses, and a maritime sector in northern Scandinavia capable of providing wood and maritime expertise. Using the innovative boat technology and warriors of northern groups, the chiefly farms of southern Scandinavia would have assumed a raiding capability that gave them a comparative advantage in trading and slaving. I posit that chieftains of the two regions became linked in confederacies, each with its own economic advantages.

As Ling, Kristiansen, and I model it, the Scandinavian Bronze Age maritime mode of production had four interlocking elements of the political economy.

Surplus Production and Investment

In both the southern and northern regions of Scandinavia, the standard Bronze Age farm was largely self-sufficient, but some surpluses were necessary to gain access to metal and other non-local resources and to other commodities produced by specialists. With access to the most productive soils, southern chiefly farms were able to produce investable surpluses to attract people, obtain trading-raiding boats, and support voyaging. To the north people were probably involved in the local trading, building, and manning of boats.

Although northern farmers probably constructed boats on their own initiative for subsistence fishing and local trading, constraints on labor and finance for larger boats would have limited their options. Surpluses in animals and grains from productive southern farms would have supported large boat construction and crewing and could explain the wealth concentrated in the hands of Thy chieftains. Their farms appear to have intensified cattle raising, probably to export cattle hides and meat for exchange. Thy's comparative advantage for exports would have been to the north, where pastureland was more marginal and high-quality flint was nonexistent.

Labor Organization of Farms and Ships

Labor on the typical farm would have been provided by its members, but to increase agriculture on chiefly farms would have required additional labor. This labor could have been servants, children of poor local farmers, or slave labor. Labor on boats was organized similarly to farms. For subsistence fishing one or two people from a farm would have been adequate. For larger boats that were involved trading and raiding, larger crews would have been necessary and inter-household relationships were essential.

As depicted in Tanum rock art, ships typically had crews of 6–13 members who would have been provided within a local chieftaincy. The largest ships represented in the rock art, however, had crews of sixty or more with defined status positions (including elevated warriors). These ships, probably accompanied by smaller boats, would have been core participants in long-distance trading and raiding sojourns, and such ships would have been the outcome of transregional confederacies. Successful Thy chieftains likely provided the large ships and support for their crews, while accompanying ships were probably financed, owned, and manned locally.

Metal Wealth

Metal wealth in Early Bronze Age Scandinavian political economy cannot be overemphasized. It provided weapons for warriors, elaborate personal equipment of male and female chiefs and warriors, and many tools for woodworking and other tasks. The magnitude of the Bronze Age metal trade was quite extraordinary. As documented by its richness, Thy's dominance of Early Bronze Age metal consumption suggests its central role in chiefly confederacies, and the means to channel wealth flows in the development of networks reliant on ownership of boats.

Exports of Amber and Slaves

To compensate for high volumes of metal and other goods imported into southern Scandinavia required a competitive advantage with high-volume valued exports from Scandinavia. What products could possibly have supported such substantial imports?

Amber is the traditional answer and the richness of amber sources in Jutland would seem to match the concentrated wealth in metal. Amber is distributed broadly in rich Bronze Age burials and loose finds throughout Europe to the Aegean. Amber is of Baltic origin and at least early in the Bronze Age most probably came primarily from Thy and other western coasts. Although highly valued in the south, quantities of metal imports to Scandinavia would have demanded a rather extraordinary export in amber. The Thy Project recovered raw amber collected for export, but in the Early Bronze Age only in small amounts. When the region abounded in rich metal finds, the most concentrated find was only one small bag with 69 pieces of raw amber. What then was the comparative advantage in Scandinavia in exports that could have allowed for rich accumulations of metal supporting chiefly confederacies?

The advantage appears to have been in its warrior might and maritime capability. The combined warrior-maritime specialty of Scandinavia would have fashioned a fearsome trading-raiding package. I propose that slaves became Scandinavia's primary exports in the emerging world system to meet labor shortages created by new regional activities throughout Europe.

As a labor commodity, slaves would have been desired by Bronze Age communities in Scandinavia—as well as farther away in urban palace societies of the eastern Mediterranean and elsewhere. Blonde northern slaves are shown in later Etruscan wall paintings, representing perhaps a continuing practice from the Bronze Age. As described comparatively for maritime chiefdoms, wealth in captive human bodies could have derived from wars and raiding. The importance of slaves in the Viking case provides the likely homology. When individuals from defeated populations were not killed, writes Stefan Brink, "They had forfeited their right to be free" (2008, p. 50).

Slaves would have been taken by those plying the coasts of Scandinavia, northern Germany, the Baltic, and elsewhere. Coastal populations would have been vulnerable to the mobile raiders described for the Viking era. Although this scenario is now speculative, as a model it provides the commodity that would have created wealth concentration; it fits the pattern of slaving described for other low-density predatory chiefdoms; and perhaps most importantly it suggests new evidence that must be obtained. New possibilities with ancient DNA would seem to be the productive route by which to investigate slavery. We envision nine features that define the maritime mode of production.

- Low-density populations interconnected by trade.
- Warriors able to raid, trade, protect, and intimidate.
- Agricultural sector with productive lands and autonomous households owned by free farmers and chieftains.
- Maritime sector with timber and specialized knowledge of boats.
- Ownership of large boats by chiefs, who supported their construction.
- Entrepreneurial voyage financed and overseen by chiefs.
- Raiding along voyaging routes for slaves and other valuables.
- Transfer of metals and slaves to boat-owning chieftains.
- Gift exchanges by chieftains to establish networks of power and alliance.

Three sources of power appear intertwined here to fashion chiefly confederacies. Positive growth cycles included the intensification of agriculture, expansion of maritime raiding-trading, accumulation and distribution of wealth, and formation of dynamic networks of power over extensive regions.

Foundational was economic power exercised through ownership of large farms and sponsorship of maritime ventures. Warrior power was instrumental to protect and extend chiefly lands and wealth and to seize slaves. Weapons attracted warriors to chiefs while these warriors also pursued their personal social advancement. And then there was ideological power, which gave meaning and legitimacy to chieftains and warrior service.

With economic surpluses chiefs could support feasts and religious specialists in ceremonies to mitigate risks of distant voyaging and warfare. Objects and actions took on special value by the ritual contexts in which they served.

PREDATORY MODES IN COMPARATIVE PERSPECTIVE

As illustrated by Scandinavia, although chiefdoms are thought to develop in high-density situations, this is not necessarily true and other examples existed worldwide. When it was possible to control flows of wealth, chiefdoms could emerge at low densities by binding together polities through exchanges of wealth. Such maritime and pastoral chiefdoms used "exclusionary" strategies to distinguish status and warriors provided the means to obtain and protect wealth. Slaves from raiding provided exchange commodities and additional labor for surplus production.

Examples of maritime chiefdoms include societies in island Southeast Asia, the Pacific, and the western coast of North America.

Southeast Asia

Illustrating maritime chiefdoms on the edge of a world system, Laura Lee Junker describes Philippine societies during the late prehistoric and early historic periods that depended on trading and slaving. She emphasizes the low population densities throughout Southeast Asia and the segmentary structure of societies.

> The Philippine archipelago became the easternmost edge of a vast network of Chinese, Southeast Asian, Indian, and Arab traders that circulated porcelains, silks, glass beads, and other luxury goods throughout the South China Sea and through the Malaccan Straits into the Indian Ocean as early as the beginning of the first millennium A.D. (1999, p. 3)

Philippine chiefdoms were not traders. Rather, they controlled exchange by creating entrepôts—channeling products, administering international trade to extract wealth, and raiding for slaves. Essential to Junker's model was the warrior nature of society that was able to initiate and maintain distant political relationships, disrupt competitors, seize and trade slaves, guarantee peaceful market transfers, and mobilize exports.

Chiefdoms supported a warrior class armed with specialized weapons obtained internationally and repurposed locally. Acquired in raids, slaves provided obligatory labor, which was relatively scarce under conditions of low population densities and little circumscription. Slave labor built and farmed pockets of intensive irrigated rice fields on Luzon that supported chiefly warriors, elites, and large port settlements. Female slaves were prestige objects involved in political exchanges to negotiate confederacies. Obtaining and protecting trade networks into Philippine interior areas channeled specialized forest products—desired by Chinese markets—through chiefly hands. Exemplifying fully developed world systems, traders were international agents who acted independently of chiefs, taxing commerce and monopolizing distributions of foreign commodities.

The Pacific

Chiefs often controlled trade by owning boats and supporting warriors to protect them. Perhaps the best examples come from Austronesian societies that spread rapidly by boat out of Taiwan as part of colonization and trade to

Melanesia, Polynesia, Micronesia, Indonesia, and coastal Malaysia and into the Indian Ocean.

Providing bottlenecks in wealth flows, ownership of boats allowed for mobile and low-cost trading and raiding. In the Pacific some chiefdoms used large seagoing canoes. A good example was the powerful maritime chiefdom located in the Roviana Lagoon in the Solomon archipelago, southeast of New Guinea. Amazing early European explorers, their war boats were large plank-built vessels with high prows; they were among the finest maritime technology ever seen in the Pacific and remarkably similar to the Hjortspring boat. These boats took 3–4 years to build, involving several stages each marked by rituals to manage high-risk, open-sea voyaging. These canoes could hold 30–60 ferocious warriors who paddled fast, often covering two hundred kilometers of open sea.

The political organization of Roviana was a hereditary chiefdom with pronounced ranking and chiefly power relied on organizing maritime headhunting expeditions. Chiefs displayed severed heads at forts and shrines to demonstrate power and call on their powerful ancestors. Headhunting expeditions also procured tradable wealth in slaves, who among other things manufactured shell valuables.

Located north of the Solomon Islands, Trobriand chiefdoms participated historically in the Kula ring trade of valuables made famous by Bronisław Malinowski. Trade voyages at sea were high risk. Every step in the manufacture of canoes and voyaging involved ritual and magic as an interwoven praxis across the landscape. At all steps chiefs mobilized food surpluses from their people to support rituals and labor. Financing boat building and voyaging, chiefs were the canoe owners and Kula valuables passed only through their hands.

Removed from the world system in the central Pacific, more complex chiefdoms and state-like polities developed based on conquest and trade. During the second millennium CE, for example, Tonga lords conquered 169 islands in their archipelago and extended hegemony over Samoa and Fiji. Large seagoing canoes owned by the chiefs allowed rapid movement over distances for carrying commodities, and of specialized warriors for surprise attacks. Slaves constituted a major part of their economy. The resulting expansive polities had profound state-like stratification, with paramount chiefs buried in massive tombs.

Desert and Steppe Chiefdoms of the Old World

Many decentralized chiefdoms depended on pastoralism and control of raiding and trading in precious commodities, including gold and slaves. On the peripheries of ancient civilizations, decentralized trading chieftaincies developed among the pastoralists of the Eurasian steppe and beyond, Arabia, and North

Africa. With the same entrepreneurial spirit as the maritime model, and with comparable mobility provided by horses and camels, pastoralist traders-raiders obtained wealth and personal status. Chiefs held advantages by owning and breeding horses and camels, navigating the ships of the desert wastes, and controlling oases that channeled wealth flows.

This conception of decentralized, pastoral chiefdoms provides an understanding of chiefly confederacies in central Asia during the Bronze and Iron ages, as they sought to control flows of metals, silks, other textiles, slaves, and additional items desired by agrarian states. After 1000 BCE steppe societies became mounted nomads and mobile as military and political forces, extending hegemony across vast regions through confederacies that would periodically develop into empires. Nikolay Kradin discusses the origin and maintenance of power by nomadic rulers, who controlled gift exchanges between independent pastoral warriors. With aspiring chiefs, nomads organized into large raiding parties that eventually formed conquest armies.

Pastoral polities were decentralized, without bureaucratic structures but always based on interpersonal relationships in a segmentary society with characteristics of the independent family unit parallel to the conception of house societies. Reminiscent of maritime chieftaincies, pastoral societies retained a dialectic between autonomy and hierarchy, decentralization and centralized authority. As described by Pekka Hämäläinen, a remarkably similar model can help understand the spread of the Comanche "empire" across America's prairies. The Comanche consisted of a weakly centralized confederacy that managed horse breeding and sought by intimidation to expand regional domination and control of trade.

THE BOTTOM LINE

Based on studying decentralized complexity of predatory chiefdoms, institutional complexity documented by unequal wealth consumption—as seen in burials—is *not* a general characteristic of chiefdoms, but rather reflects the significance of controlled wealth circulation in political economies. In simple terms, chiefdoms are recognized not by any general list of traits defining regional polities, but by the varying characteristics of their political economies that allow for mobilization and allocation of surpluses.

Raiding and trading societies with a predatory modality depend on segmentary social structures—with strong initiatives from the house group—and on the strong attraction of wealth and weapons. Critical is mobility provided by boats and mounted animals, which serve both for rapid logistical movement and transport of bulk commodities. Mobility and transport are essential for developing the raiding-trading complex (typically linked to slaving) that depends on long-distance movements of goods and people, especially linked to world systems of trade.

To the degree leaders can exert control over these commodity flows by owning transport technology or nodal trading points, they can channel flows of wealth and weapons sufficient to develop networks of dependency that support centralizing power. But these chiefdoms are unstable and dependent on many factors that shift routes and commodities, resulting in rapid development and collapse of chiefdoms. Predatory chiefdoms thus represent one end of a spectrum of emergent political systems that cycles rapidly and unpredictably, in contrast to the opposite end of chiefdoms that depend on intensified agricultural production of surpluses from engineered environments.

ADDITIONAL READINGS

Bech, Jens-Herik, Berit Valentin Eriksen, and Kristian Kristiansen (editors). 2018. *Bronze Age Settlement and Land-Use in Thy, Northwest Denmark*. 2 vols. Højbjerg, Denmark: Aarhus University Press. Monograph presents the full description of the Thy Archaeological Project used as the primary data set to construct the model of southern Scandinavian chiefdoms dependent on surplus production in chiefly farms.

Beck, Robin A. 2007 (editor). *The Durable House: House Society Models in Archaeology*. Occasional Paper No. 35, Center for Archaeological Investigations, Southern Illinois University, Carbondale. Edited book describing house societies with examples from around the world. Of particular importance is the social inequality based on ownership of productive resources. The chapter by Douglas Bolender argues for the applicability of house society to Viking Iceland.

Clark, Geoffrey, David V. Burley, and Timothy Murray. 2008. Monumentality and the Development of the Tongan Maritime Chiefdom. *Antiquity* 82:994–1008. Article describes the Tonga chiefdom-states based on maritime conquest and trade in the central Pacific.

Earle, Timothy, Johan Ling, Claes Uhner, Zofia Stos-Gale, and Lene Melheim. 2015. The Political Economy and Metal Trade in Bronze Age Europe: Understanding Regional Variability in Terms of Comparative Advantages and Articulations. *European Journal of Archaeology* 18:633–657. Argues that regional variability in Bronze Age societies was based on comparative advantages of exports (like tin and copper), technologies of trade (especially seaworthy boats), and control over transport routes. Article illustrates the meaning of a bottleneck as relevant to prestige good modalities.

Gilman, Antonio. 1995. Prehistoric European Chiefdoms: Rethinking "Germanic" Societies. In *Foundations of Social Inequality*, edited by T. Douglas

Price and Gary M. Feinman, pp. 235–251. New York: Plenum. Gilman describes the Germanic mode of production derived from Marx and used to understand European political economies.

Hämäläinen, Pekka. 2008. *The Comanche Empire*. New Haven, CT: Yale University Press. A fine case study of the historic Comanche "empire," an extensive chieftaincy based on control of horse breeding, intimidation by raiding, and control of trade relationships (especially guns) with European colonial societies.

Hasslöf, Olaf. 1970. *Sømand, Fisker, Skib og Værft: Introduktion til Maritim Etnologi* [Sailor, Fisherman, Ship and Shipyard: Introduction to Maritime Ethnology]. Copenhagen: Rosenkilde & Bagger. Monograph describes the importance of boats in Scandinavian society with estimates of the specifics for the Iron Age Hjortspring boat from southern Denmark, which provides a model for the Bronze Age crafts of Scandinavia.

Kristiansen, Kristian. 2002. The Tale of the Sword: Swords and Swordfighters in Bronze Age Europe. *Oxford Journal of Archaeology* 21:319–332. Kristiansen conducted use-wear analyses of Bronze Age swords, showing that they were of two functional types: warrior swords with extensive fighting damage and resharpening, and ornate chiefly swords with no fighting damage but with wear showing their use in dress.

Kristiansen, Kristian, and Timothy Earle. In preparation. Modeling Modes of Production: European Third and Second Millennium BC Economies. Kristiansen and I summarize the Bronze Age economies of Europe. These economies were integrated internationally but showed distinctive local patterns of development, representing their articulation with the bronze trade.

Ling. Johan. 2014. *Elevated Rock Art: Towards a Maritime Understanding of Bronze Age Rock Art in Northern Bohuslän, Sweden*. Oxford, UK: Oxbow. Ling's doctoral dissertation looks at the archaeological sequence of Tanum in Bohuslän, Sweden. Focus is on the maritime economy especially represented in the World Heritage rock art sites of Tanum.

Ling, Johan, Timothy Earle, and Kristian Kristiansen. 2018. Maritime Mode of Production: Raiding and Trading in Seafaring Chiefdoms. *Current Anthropology* 59:488–524. This article lays out the logic and evidence for the maritime mode of production discussed in this chapter.

Malinowski, Bronisław. 1922. *Argonauts of the Western Pacific*. London: Routledge & Kegan Paul. Malinowski was an ethnographer among the British structural functionalists. His monograph on the Trobriand Islands is an anthropological classic looking at the role of chiefs in the inter-island Kula trade that functioned to maintain social hierarchy. Chiefs supported manufacture of seaworthy crafts, which they owned.

Price, Neil. 2016. Pirates of the North Sea? The Viking Ship as a Political Space. In *Comparative Perspectives on Past Colonisation: Maritime Interaction and Cultural Integration*, edited by Lene Melheim, Hakon Glørstad, and Zanette Tsigaridas Glørstad, pp. 149–176. Sheffield, UK: Equinox. Price describes the maritime role of raiding and trading in the Viking economy. Perhaps most important is his emphasis on the slave trade in Viking society.

Sweet, Louise. 1965. Camel Raiding of North African Bedouin: A Mechanism of Ecological Adaptation. *American Anthropologist* 67:1132–1150. Sweet describes the raiding-trading complex of Arab pastoralists. The society was segmentary, organized by family units (camps) with high degrees of personal initiative in raiding and trading. Chiefs were able to control trade—especially in slaves—by ownership of oases.

CHAPTER 8

MODELS FOR ARCHAEOLOGICAL RESEARCH ON CHIEFDOMS

Chiefdoms document sociopolitical processes by which leaders expand sovereignty over populations in the thousands. Chiefs are effective political actors able to fashion control over a new scale of human organization (beyond the kin-based village). Chiefdoms are highly variable in both stability and extent, but they represent regional institutionalization of power and authority. They were the first political machines, not a societal type.

CHIEFDOMS: ARCHAEOLOGY'S EXCEPTIONAL OPPORTUNITY

Chiefdoms can be understood as foundational to the origin of states and continue to operate politically within states. Questions of how and why chiefdoms emerged can be understood empirically by anthropological archaeology; we alone have the data for comparative diachronic studies. Social evolution has been and continues to be a longstanding theme in anthropology. No topic in the social sciences is so uniquely suited to anthropological archaeology as the emergence of regional political institutions.

To understand chiefdoms is to understand power. I identify three intertwined sources of elemental power—religious ideology, warrior might, and economy. Chiefdoms are highly variable as a suite of middle-range societies that have gone by many names. I call them all chiefdoms because they involve the formation of regional leadership that is at least partially institutionalized. The formations of chiefdoms are, however, highly variable based on particular political strategies that creatively mix elemental sources of power. Their variability is no greater than that seen in states formed out of chiefdoms.

I take a particular stand that contrasting chiefly strategies are common processes involving control of political economies to provide material support for ruling institutions. Simply stated, to study chiefdoms we must understand how resources are mobilized and distributed to concentrate power regionally. The different ways may be modeled as alternative modes of production. These economic modalities represent processes by which economic flows may be channeled to finance political institutions. Any specific case will combine these processes in different ways so that all the modes grade into each other as strategies are combined to form real political finance. The different processes of these modalities are useful as models to provide test implications for archaeological research. Other sociocultural factors certainly have independent dynamics, but they link to these modal processes.

FOUR MODES OF PRODUCTION IN CHIEFDOMS

I identify four modes of production that represent rather distinctive pathways that the regional organization of chiefdoms developed. They represent different power strategies linked to contrasting opportunities for control. The ritual, corporate, and Asiatic modalities are a continuum of increasing agricultural intensification supporting larger settled populations and surplus mobilization. The predatory mode of production is distinct, creating examples of low-density chiefly societies based on regional networks formed by the centralized distribution of wealth objects.

Commonly, the primary bottleneck is productive land improved with landesque capital. Based on the chiefly financed engineered landscapes, chiefdoms can assume characteristics of increased scale and institutional formations that come to be associated with states. This increasing institutional complexity appears to be linked to expanding control over surpluses by warrior conquest and/or articulation with the world system.

Ritual Mode of Production

First, apparently both chronologically and foundationally, is the ritual mode of production. I illustrate this with the Early Neolithic of southern Scandinavia and the Late Archaic and Woodland periods of the southeastern United States. Many researchers would deny that chiefdoms exist during these times, but I propose that the regional, institutional aspect characterizes group-oriented chiefdoms. The key process involved in the ritual mode of production is building ritual places with social labor. These places hold monument architecture that provides permanency of place.

Small-scale construction activities can be accomplished by small kin-ordered groups, but the expansion to monument scale engages larger work parties mobilized from regional populations. To the degree that leaders are involved in construction activities and associated ceremonies (indicated by scale and task complexity), leaders can assume ritual power. As the basis of an emergent political economy, the ability of leaders to mobilize and compensate labor is based on chiefly roles linked to overarching property rights that allow accumulating surpluses. The bottleneck is the property rights asserted by the chief's sponsorship to build the ritual landscape and support group ceremonies at the monuments.

The essential archaeological indicator of the ritual mode of production is the scale and tempo of labor invested in monument construction. But what is the actual documentation of chiefs? Ethnographically, chiefs organize such labor for ritual constructions beyond the scale of a village ritual house. Societies associated with ritual monuments are also associated with non-local ritual objects. These objects from afar are easier for chiefs to control than locally procured objects, and chiefs act to supersede local ceremonial objects with distant ones as a means to create bottlenecks to express sacred meaning. Thus the objects themselves, often found in ritual contexts but sometimes directly associated with individuals, probably document chiefly (priestly) powers.

Corporate Mode of Production

Second is the corporate mode of production, which is also basic to early societies as they emerge at higher population densities in village communities. I illustrate this modality with hillfort chiefdoms of highland Peru and Iron Age Europe. Many researchers believe that chiefdoms did not exist in these societies, and often they are correct. Mutual defense of small-scale communities does not require much leadership, but it can offer opportunities for war leaders to emerge as defensive requirements increased.

The key process again involves the creation of corporate property held by groups and based on the capital invested in landscapes. With uneven population growth— typical of small populations—the distribution of land with respect to population can easily become unbalanced, and competition intensifies as larger groups seek opportunities to take land from weaker neighbors. Local groups construct elaborate defensive works for protection, but also to assert property rights—a willingness to stand their ground. In some cases the scale of defensive works increases to require labor comparable to monument construction in the ritual modality.

Tunanmarca's polity illustrates how a central defensive site with ten thousand inhabitants is able to dominate a regional settlement hierarchy. To the degree that leaders organize construction of defensive works, associated social labor ceremonies, and actual defensive actions, leaders can become warrior chiefs with generalizing authority. As the basis of an emergent political economy, the ability of leaders to mobilize and compensate labor for construction is based on overarching rights to surpluses materialized by fortified central places. The bottleneck is the defensive landscape of corporately held lands with rights to surpluses.

The essential archaeological indicator of the corporate modality is the scale and tempo of labor invested in defensive works, and the settlement hierarchy incorporating a regional population in the thousands. Scales of construction require labor coordination and the power of the largest centers cannot be resisted easily by neighboring villages. In some situations increasing importance of specialized weaponry is a source of power. Ritual power can be of little significance in the archaeological record of such societies. Objects from afar seem rarely to distinguish the status of chiefs, who appear archaeologically as first among equals within an egalitarian ethos. The primary source of power is military dominance, with surplus mobilization tied to chiefly ability to mobilize surpluses from the populations they help defend.

Asiatic Mode of Production

Third is the Asiatic mode of production. The classic cases discussed here are the Polynesian chiefdoms dependent especially on extensive irrigation complexes, but removed from or prior to emergent world systems. Hawaiian chiefdoms provide a remarkable case of how such polities can take on statelike characteristics without markets or cities. Many other cases of chiefdoms based on these engineered agricultural facilities exist throughout the world—including the city-states or small kingdoms of the Middle East, Egypt, Mesoamerica, and Peru.

The essential archaeological indicators of the Asiatic mode of production are the scale and tempo of labor invested in productive facilities that generate surpluses supporting ruling institutions. Centralized storage often documents the associated staple finance. Central places in regional settlement hierarchies are typically associated with major ritual monuments—stages for legitimizing ceremonies. Additionally, objects are associated with this modality as a means to distinguish chiefs as a ruling class with religious sanctity and warrior might. Although the primary source of power is ownership of engineered landscapes, this ownership requires both ritual legitimation and warrior might to seize and hold productive facilities.

Predatory Mode of Production

Fourth is the predatory mode of production, which I illustrate with the Scandinavian Bronze and Iron Age societies on the periphery of Europe. Other cases include maritime chiefdoms of island Southeast Asia and the pastoral societies across the Asian steppes, the Arabian peninsula, and Saharan North Africa. Researchers generally accept these societies as chiefdoms based on their political hierarchies, unequal distribution of wealth, and regional organization. Leaders are identified both ethnographically and archaeologically. A warrior elite dominates predatory raids in addition to active trade.

The key processes of the predatory modality appear to be quite different from land-based political economies. The objective is to control wealth flows creating the prestige goods economies of interdependency. Increased differentiation of chiefs represents their relative independence from local revenue sources.

Chiefs establish control by warrior might over wealth-based political economies, often at considerable distances. Bottlenecks include the technology for rapid movement of wealth, used by traders and raiders to obtain and protect high-value items. The chieftains' ownership of productive lands may also be important to gain control over the technology for mobility and warrior dominance. Additionally, chieftains assert ownership over points of movement including harbors, rivers, mountain passes, and oases. Critical to this modality appears to be the relatively high volume of wealth trade, typically as articulation with world systems. Predatory modes are quite limited in the New World, apparently because of the relatively lower volume of distant trade and less-developed technologies of transport.

The main archaeological indicators for predatory modality are high-volume and distant flows of wealth and weapons distributed broadly but unequally in burials and chiefly houses. Special weaponry, often made of foreign materials worked by attached specialists, characterizes these chiefdoms. Remarkably, however, these societies exist at lower population densities and have little investment in monument architecture and few or no settlement hierarchies than are often thought to characterize chiefdoms. Monument construction is usually limited to personal facilities including chiefly burials and houses. Group monuments are not typical.

MODALITIES AS PROCESSUAL MODELS OF THE POLITICAL ECONOMY

Importantly, these four modalities of political economies are not political types but processual models of how economic flows can be channeled to support power relationships in ritual, warfare, and surplus production. The specifics of any society are historically determined and highly idiosyncratic; political economies represent continuous variability in the social formations that we observe ethnographically and archaeologically.

Having said this, by modeling alternative modalities we can identify the strategies by which surpluses were mobilized and invested in sources of power in order to construct alternative institutional formations. In all, chiefdoms are not of one or even multiple types. They are highly variable, regionally structured political societies with contrasting strategies for power concentration. Importantly, the marking of chiefs does not necessarily involve concentrated wealth; instead it is often materialized in the built landscape.

The summaries of four chiefly modalities emphasize how chiefs act in alternative and creative ways. This top-down consideration underscores political processes but does not adequately stress other essential characteristics of

human societies. Human societies operate as multiscalar organizations em-
bedding individuals, families, and communities within a regional polity. When
a new level of integration is created, the existing organizational forms are not
replaced; rather, they continue to serve preexisting functions, but characteristically with some altered means. Thus families continue to operate within
village-scale communities and the communities continue to operate as part of
regional chiefdoms.

To understand the totality of chiefly societies requires understanding the
constituent parts—families and kin-structured communities, each with their
own agency, organizational forms, and operational logic. With the formation
of regional chiefdoms, most activities of everyday life and well-being continue to be handled just fine at these non-chiefly scales.

Although agency is established regionally through chiefly action, separate goals, agency, and independent actions continue at community and household levels. These levels can often be best understood through anarchistic
theories. Chiefdoms incorporate their constituent parts by providing services
either real or imagined.

- The ritual modes provide identity and meaning to local kin-
  ordered groups.
- Corporate modes provide protection of property rights in land.
- Asiatic modes construct and maintain highly productive and
  sustainable agricultural facilities.
- Predatory modes circulate wealth and weapons for individual
  status and defense.

As captured by collective action theory, although chiefs and rulers seek to
maximize revenues and power, their abilities to do it depend on fulfilling goals
of constituent individuals and groups. Power in the hands of the people—
whether farmers, sailors, or warriors—determines the possibilities open to
leaders.

CODA: WHERE HAVE ALL THE CHIEFS GONE?

To understand how states operate today, we can consider how ancient states
developed from chiefdoms and eventually formed modern state societies. With
the evolution of states, chiefs did not disappear; to the contrary, they adapted
creatively to state governance, retaining many previous power dynamics. A
true understanding of states must consider how chief-like actors became sub-
state agents.

Medieval Europe documents the formation of states by forceful incorporation of chiefly actors and eventual restructuring of political economies. At
the collapse of the western Roman Empire, the integration of administration

and military systems crumbled throughout Europe and the political economy returned to staple-based feudal estates. These were chiefdom-like units like the hillfort chiefdoms that Rome had conquered, but with a historical tradition of social stratification. Local chiefs ("lords") lived in castles and attracted warriors able to assert ownership over agrarian estates worked by peasant serfs. In return for access to subsistence plots, serfs provided labor to support their lords.

As represented by Charlemagne (king of France and first Holy Roman emperor), paramount chiefs were sometimes able to defeat local lords and extract from them support in wars of conquest. A quick look at the archaeological signature of such "states" shows how minimally institutionalized they actually were. When I went to see Charlemagne's capital at Aachen in western Germany, I was struck by how small an affair it actually was—some courtly buildings and a beautiful (but small) Christian shrine. Control of labor materialized in monument construction was limited. Charlemagne's state and empire were fragile affairs, comparable to prehistoric chiefdoms.

With expanding political economies based on markets, trade, and urbanism, kings in the late medieval period established relatively centralized institutional power. But lordly castles continued to stand against centralized power. French kings often felt threatened to move outside Paris, fearful of the lords of the countryside. These chief-like actors with their independent estates continued to be foundational to feudalism, and kings had to encourage or coerce loyalty.

Failed States or Successful Chiefdoms?

Georgi Derlugian and I look at how modern chief-like actors retain substantial power both in collaboration and in conflict with states. What we call the myth of the modern state suggests that such traits of states as territorial control, monopoly of force, and effective judiciaries and bureaucracies are often elusive. Using these measures, all states are in some sense failing. Idealized principles of state governance are perhaps only the unrealized dream of state authorities. Rather, modern states are always patched-together institutions with uneven sovereignty over space and activities. Chiefs thrive in the interstitial spaces of states, acting according to their own interests. These chiefs go by many names—oligarchs, local political bosses, drug lords, and gang leaders.

The American Revolution created a "failed" state by rebelling against the British monarchy. Acting much as chiefs, American traders and plantation owners supported an army that fought for the freedom to enrich themselves. To maintain a political economy free of monarchist and parliamentary oversight and regulation, colonists supported the right to trade freely and own slaves—the two greatest sources of wealth in colonial America.

The American Revolution can be seen as a rebellion by loosely organized chiefs at the peripheries of imperial governance. American ideology stressed principles encapsulated in the free market and the Bill of Rights. Framers of the Constitution saw advantages to restrain state power and sought limits on intrusion into local affairs, where politicians, farmers, and traders could act without state regulation. Over the last two hundred years, the laws of the land have developed fitfully to channel these freedoms for the general good. America represents the power retained by chief-like agents to maintain personal interests.

Taming Chiefs in Modern States

Within modern states chiefs act with anarchistic powers that challenge, subvert, and sometimes replace existing states. Forming a stable and functioning modern state depends on balancing interests and power of constituent agents, much as earlier chiefdoms and archaic states had to do at lower levels of integration. For a modern state to operate requires the taming of chiefs. Chieftaincies reach up to the state to corrupt legal structures, but the state also reaches down to use its embedded chieftains to outsource state responsibility (as was seen dramatically in the recent reactions to the pandemic). Mafia dons, drug lords, oligarchs, and local political figures within states morph their identity and power in negotiation with state institutions.

The goal of sub-state chieftains is to create freedom to operate with minimum oversight. The goal of the state is to tame and sometimes co-opt the aggressive and creative initiative of chiefs, whose ability to maneuver quickly around restraining actions is legendary. Truly effective modern states would appear to require two things: first, recognizing the inherent power of sub-state actors to operate only in their interests; and second, maintaining a strong rule of law to tame chiefs to act also for the broad societal good.

Business and government leaders in modern states operate much like chiefs, largely outside state objectives. As described by Jeffrey Winters, oligarchs amass great wealth, use their wealth to corrupt government officials, create favorable laws, and hire a cadre of lawyers (modern warriors) to defend their wealth and power. Even presidents act more like chiefs than presidents, using personal loyalty to circumvent established laws. Perhaps you have noticed.

Functions within the state are difficult for the state to manage or control directly. These are given over to chief-like entrepreneurs who can govern outside state laws. Administering the patchwork of regions and localities within a state proves to be almost impossible. Modern states include expanding spheres of dense urban cores, surrounding rural areas, and distant regions, in which the state is often only symbolic or irregular. Modern chiefs, each with distinctive characteristics, operate within these spheres of the state: corrupt government officials within the core, weakly controlled regional governors, and distantly allied operatives. These chiefs—like their prehistoric forebears—hold opportunistic, personal, and non-bureaucratic power. For a comparative anthropological archaeologist, these patterns are both expected and understandable.

Archaeologists studying chiefdoms provide critical insight into studying political actors. We have a limitless number of natural experiments (our regional chronologies) that show the long-term implications of different political configuration. Perhaps acting as chiefs controlling key resources, archaeologists have this extraordinary database that we must learn to exploit. Archaeologists can offer an important historical perspective within the social sciences to understand the dynamics of social chance. We are of major relevance to anthropology within both academia and policy discourse.

ADDITIONAL READINGS

Derlugian, Georgi, and Timothy Earle. 2010. Strong Chieftaincies Out of Weak States, or Elemental Power Unbound. *Comparative Social Research* 27:27–51. Working with historical sociologist Georgi Derlugian, I look at the dynamic character of sub-state chief-like actors responsible in modern states. The paper resulted from a conference and special issue on failed states in the developing world.

Winters, Jeffrey A. 2011. *Oligarchy*. New York: Cambridge University Press. Winters uses the anthropological concept of chiefs to understand modern oligarchs (incredibly wealthy individuals) who have outsized roles in many modern societies. His two primary cases are twentieth century Indonesia and the United States.

PROJECT
STUDYING A CHIEFDOM

You are asked to analyze the available evidence for the political economy and social formations in an intermediate-level society (chiefdom). The goal is to describe and understand a single archaeological case from among examples chosen by your professor. Your job is to consider a range of variables that are commonly associated with chiefdoms. These combine in sundry ways to create chiefly modalities; do not expect all variables to be present or of significance in any case. The purpose of your systematic description is to be able to suggest the modality of the political economy that resulted in a particular chiefly formation. This analysis requires comparison with the different modes of production described in Chapters 4–7.

Please refer to Chapter 3 for how to measure pertinent variables. The most important variables for you to consider are:

- Regional settlement hierarchy.
- Monument architecture.
- Nature and distribution of wealth objects in burials and other contexts.
- Nature and distribution of defensive works and weapons.

In your consideration of these variables, you will identify the particular mix of the primary "currencies" in the economy (labor, prestige goods, and weapons). It is critical for you to understand the economy as flows in these factors and to suggest the possible bottlenecks in the system that allow them to be channeled centrally or not, as the case may be. Here you will want to consider difficulties in controlling the economic organization of different social scales—the family (house), community, and regional polity.

In considering economic flows and their bottlenecks, you will seek to describe the political economy and how it results in control—or lack thereof—for the elemental sources of power. These powers are the economy (land, labor, and capital), warrior might, and religious ideology. Any chief tries to maximize centralized power by creating particular strategies that mix and connect these possible sources.

Most important is to describe contrasts between labor invested in engineered landscapes (religious monuments, defensive works, and economic facilities), means of developing property, and the production, distribution, and consumption of objects of distinction. The purpose is to understand how the particular case you are studying relates to the four modes of production that have been presented. Remember these modalities are not sociopolitical types, but rather represent processes of control and resistance that create historical originality in each society studied.

REFERENCES

Bernardini, Wesley. 2004. Hopewell Geometric Earthworks: A Case Study in the Referential and Experiential Meaning of Monuments. *Journal of Anthropological Archaeology* 23:331–356.

Blanton, Richard E., and Lane F. Fargher. 2008. *Collective Action in the Formation of Pre-Modern States*. New York: Springer.

Brink, Stefan. 2008. Slavery in the Viking Age. In *The Viking World*, edited by Stefan Brink and Neil Price, pp. 49–56. London: Routledge.

Dalberg-Acton, John. 1895. *A Lecture on the Study of History*. London: Macmillan.

Engels, Friedrich. 1883. Speech at the Grave of Karl Marx, March 22. *MIA Encyclopedia of Marxism*. (online)

Falconer, Steven E., and Stephen H. Savage. 2009. The Bronze Age Political Landscape of the Southern Levant. In *Polities and Power: Archaeological Perspectives on the Landscapes of Early States*, edited by Steven E. Falconer and Charles L. Redman, pp. 125–151. Tucson: University of Arizona Press.

Firth, Raymond. 1936. *We the Tikopia: A Sociological Study of Kinship in Primitive Polynesia*. London: George Allen & Unwin.

Hastorf, Christine A., and Timothy Earle. 1985. Intensive Agriculture and the Geography of Political Change in the Upper Mantaro Region, Peru. In *Prehistoric Intensive Agriculture in the Tropics*, edited by I. S. Farrington, pp. 569–595. BAR International Series No. 232. Oxford, UK: Archaeopress.

168 References

Junker, Laura Lee. 1999. *Raiding, Trading, and Feasting: The Political Economy of Philippine Chiefdoms*. Honolulu: University of Hawaii Press.

Lowie, Robert H. 1920. *Primitive Society*. New York: Boni & Liveright.

Mintz, Sidney. 2014. And the Rest Is History: A Conversation with Sidney Mintz by Jonathan Thomas. *American Anthropologist* 116:497–510.

Price, Neil. 2016. Pirates of the North Sea? The Viking Ship as a Political Space. In *Comparative Perspectives on Past Colonisation: Maritime Interaction and Cultural Integration*, edited by Lene Melheim, Hakon Glørstad, and Zanette Tsigaridas Glørstad, pp. 149–176. Sheffield, UK: Equinox.

Steward, Julian H. 1955. *Theory of Culture Change: The Methodology of Multilinear Evolution*. Urbana: University of Illinois Press.

Trigger, Bruce. 1990. Monumental Architecture: A Thermodynamic Explanation of Symbolic Behaviour. *World Archaeology* 22:119–132.